# LOVE
# LEADERSHIP

# LOVE LEADERSHIP

## THE NEW WAY TO LEAD
## IN A FEAR-BASED WORLD

John Hope Bryant

FOREWORD BY BILL GEORGE

JOSSEY-BASS
A Wiley Imprint
www.josseybass.com

Published by Jossey-Bass
A Wiley Imprint
989 Market Street, San Francisco, CA 94103-1741—www.josseybass.com

Jossey-Bass books and products are available through most bookstores. To contact Jossey-Bass directly call our Customer Care Department within the U.S. at 800-956-7739, outside the U.S. at 317-572-3986, or fax 317-572-4002.

Jossey-Bass also publishes its books in a variety of electronic formats. Some content that appears in print may not be available in electronic books.

**Library of Congress Cataloging-in-Publication Data**

Bryant, John.
  Love leadership : the new way to lead in a fear-based world / John Hope Bryant; foreword by Bill George.—1st ed.
      p. cm.
  Includes bibliographical references and index.
  ISBN 978-0-470-42878-8 (cloth)
  1. Leadership. 2. Interpersonal relations. 3. Success. I. Title.
  HD57.7.B786 2009
  303.3'4—dc22

                                                                    2009020137

Printed in the United States of America
FIRST EDITION
*HB Printing*     10 9 8 7 6 5 4 3 2 1

*To Bill Robinson, founding program manager of Operation HOPE, Chicago, who recruited hundreds of volunteers, educated thousands of young bright minds, and showed us all how to live a life that "gets" by giving.*

*To Secretary Jack Kemp, your words and deeds demonstrate the stand you took for those "less than," and you will never be forgotten. You were the Republican that everyone could talk to.*

*You both have been promoted.*

# CONTENTS

Contents

# FOREWORD

I doubt that you have ever read anything quite like this marvelous book by John Hope Bryant. Lest you're misled by the title and think that *Love Leadership* represents the "soft side" of leadership, let me assure you that love leadership is hard. Very hard.

Being a command-and-control leader who issues orders and overpowers people isn't difficult, and it isn't leadership. It is coercion.

Throughout my career, I have observed many who use fear as a leadership style to take advantage of people and to control and manipulate them. As we see every day by the failures of these leaders—from Wall Street firms like Lehman Brothers and Bear Stearns to companies like Chrysler and Health South—they cannot sustain success in the twenty-first century by leading with fear.

People who lead by coercion will never empower people to peak performance over a sustained period of time. Eventually the best people leave the organization, and others just capitulate. Over time, performance declines, and so does the organization.

When I worked for Litton Industries in the 1970s as president of Litton Microwave Cooking, the corporation's new CEO used fear and coercion as his primary style. One day when we were touring the machine shop, he verbally accosted a machine tool worker, yelling at him about the metal scraps coming out of his machine. The worker was taken aback and didn't know how to respond, but he certainly wasn't motivated.

Later that same day, the CEO started shouting in a meeting at our vice president of human resources about the division's benefits policies. I intervened to say that I had approved these policies and that if he objected to them, he should direct his concerns to me. In my office after the meeting, I expressed concern that his intimidating style had a negative impact on our staff. He replied, "Bill, this is the only style I have used throughout my career, and it works for me."

Incidents like these were common among twentieth-century leaders. The media contributed to the problem by venerating so-called tough bosses like Donald Trump with mantras like "You're fired." Leaders like this aren't really tough, as much as they are tyrants and bullies who use their power to take advantage of other people.

My experiences with today's leaders have led me to believe that in the twenty-first century, love leadership—

described by Bryant as the opposite of leading with fear—is the only kind of leadership that can sustain success.

In the twentieth century, people looked to all-powerful leaders with legions of followers, whom they trusted and to whom they gave their loyalty. All too often, these leaders betrayed their trust. In the twenty-first century, trust must be earned by the leader before loyalty is conveyed by the people. It is in crises that people look to their leaders to determine if they are authentic and follow their True North.

Today's leaders must be very different, because their people have changed. Their organizations are filled with knowledge workers who know more than their bosses. These workers want to step up and lead now rather than waiting in line for ten to twenty years. Why shouldn't they have that opportunity? I was division general manager of Litton's microwave business at twenty-seven years old. If young people don't get opportunities like that, they will likely move on.

Most of all, these days people are looking for meaning and significance in their work, not just compensation. If people are going to devote more time to their work than any other aspect of their lives, they feel they have a right to find meaning in it.

To quote Dave Dillon, chair and CEO of Kroger, from my book, *True North*, "All human beings want to find meaning in their lives. At Kroger we're aligned in believing that serving the public is a dignified, proud profession.

We make customers' lives better because someone is friendly and helpful to them. Little touches of human kindness can literally change their day. Employees delivering human kindness feel better about their work. At the end of their careers, they can say, 'I was part of something special.'"

Love leaders understand at a deeper level how to bring out the best in people and empower them to perform at far higher levels of performance than anyone believes is possible. *Love leadership*, however, isn't about singing "Kum-Ba-Yah" around the campfire. Bryant has a much deeper and more insightful understanding of what it means to lead with love.

He describes why leading with love means learning from loss and failure, and shares personal stories about his own challenges. He demonstrates convincingly why being vulnerable gives you power, offering moving stories of what it means to be vulnerable, and how your vulnerability as a leader enables you to connect with people at a deeper level.

One of the most poignant examples comes from the time he invited Alan Greenspan, then the chairman of the Federal Reserve, to a middle school classroom in inner-city Washington, D.C. Bryant suggested to Greenspan that he set aside his prepared remarks and speak from his heart. According to Bryant, the chairman of the Federal Reserve just talked about his life, going back to his childhood, and related it to the current challenges he faced. The students were deeply motivated by Greenspan's message: "If I can do it, you can do it."

Throughout this book, Bryant teaches with stories like this one. He demonstrates that "When you get real with people, when you show vulnerability, you connect with them and you move them on a human level. That gives you real power. . . . People meet you where you are. If you're open, they tend to be open. If you're closed, they tend to be closed. If you're vulnerable, they tend to be vulnerable."

In my experience, it's not easy to be vulnerable when people are looking to you as their leader, but it is much more effective. Sharing your story with people in ways that exposes your vulnerability connects you deeply with others and enables you to form authentic relationships. When you do that, people will trust you and be willing to align with your leadership goals and your values.

Bryant shows how leading with love is central to career success and describes why the expression of love in business—creating long-term relationships with your customers, employees, and community, based on caring for others and doing good—makes you wealthy. He contends that giving is really getting. As he says, "Leaders give—followers take. . . . Giving inspires loyalty, attracts good people, confers peace of mind, and lies at the core of true wealth."

John Bryant's message is powerful, and it's one we can learn from. But the best thing about John Bryant is that he doesn't just preach this message: he *lives* it.

I have watched him reach out to a very powerful person, telling him, "You have a big heart, but you cover your humanity with your intellect. Why don't you just let your hair down and let people see the real you?" Most of us, myself included, would be afraid to be so direct for fear of harming the relationship. Yet people accept this kind of feedback from John because they know he cares about them.

If you want to become an authentic leader, John Hope Bryant will show you how. He has been through the depths and come back. Through the challenges he faced, Bryant learned how to become a leader who can change the world.

Trust me: John Bryant *is* changing the world.

Growing up in a tough environment in south Los Angeles, he was exposed to gangs, drug dealers, and pimps, but was able to avoid them all. He started out as a teenage entrepreneur, and lost it all on a failed venture. Bryant wound up as a homeless man, living in his Jeep for six months. That's where he decided he wanted to make a difference in the world around him.

In 2002, Bryant was called to action by the race riots that followed the acquittal of the L.A. policemen who beat Rodney King. He saw how financial services organizations took advantage of poor people, exploiting their lack of financial literacy through what he terms "ghettoized financial services." In response, he organized a group of local bankers to go into the south Los Angeles neighborhood where he grew up, and study how they could help the poor people living there.

The following year, Bryant founded Operation HOPE to help poor people across America attain financial literacy. Since that time, he has raised over $500 million for this cause. Through Operation HOPE, he is addressing the problems of financial services organizations taking advantage of poor people with misleading home mortgages and credit card scams.

But John Bryant didn't stop there. In April 2007, he took his cause to then president George W. Bush and key members of his cabinet. He explained how the poor were vulnerable to being ripped off in a multitude of ways by their lack of financial literacy. In January 2008, President Bush responded by creating the U.S. President's Advisory Council on Financial Literacy, with a time frame that would carry over into the next president's term. Bush selected Charles Schwab, the founder of Charles Schwab & Company, to chair the council, and asked Bryant to become its vice chair.

*Love Leadership* is not so much about John Bryant's leadership as it is about *your* leadership—how you can lead with love instead of fear and become a much more effective leader in this process.

Through love leadership, people will give fully—mind, body, heart, and spirit—to your organization in order to accomplish challenging goals, rather than just doing the minimum required of them. This is the way twenty-first-century leaders empower people and achieve peak performance. In my experience, an organization of empowered leaders will outperform a top-down, command-and-control organization every time.

Most important of all, love leadership is not just a better way to lead but a more fulfilling way to live. At the end of the day, love leaders know they have lived their lives with integrity; developed authentic, lasting relationships; and enhanced every environment they have been in by their presence. That alone makes it all worthwhile.

*June 2009*                                          Bill George
                                          *Author of* True North

# LOVE
# LEADERSHIP

# INTRODUCTION:
# FROM FEAR TO HOPE

G rowing up in the inner city in Southern California, I remember being surrounded by fear. Intimidation hung thick in the air. No one dared pass through the street behind our house in the city of Compton, near Los Angeles. Criminals had hijacked a community filled with ambitious, loving, hardworking people. If you didn't know who you were, someone else was willing to tell you, and there were consequences for not listening.

The pressure to join a gang was constant. Thugs all around me thought of their gang as their "family," a concept I could respect and even admire, if only the family silverware didn't have your elderly neighbor's name stamped on it.

I remember a local punk nicknamed Tweet, who lived next door to me. He was ninety-seven pounds wet, but scared the living daylights out of everyone in the neighborhood.

I also remember my best friend, George, who lived down the street from me. He was eighteen, and I was ten. George was a polite, straight-A student, but the problem with George was that for some reason he thought being like Tweet was actually cooler. So George hung around Tweet, then began to dress like Tweet, and eventually to walk and talk like Tweet.

My mother, however, said no way to dressing like or hanging out with Tweet or anyone else. Groups of people don't succeed, she told me—individuals do. She didn't want me being a part of any group, at least not until I knew how to think for myself. She didn't compel me with a lecture, but rather through her presence. I had absolutely no opportunity to join a gang. She went everywhere with me, and took me everywhere with her. The only gang she would let me join was hers.

Like many people when I was growing up, we didn't have a lot of money, so my mother augmented that lack with a lot of invested time and love. She made all our toys and clothes. But these clothes weren't anything like "the uniform," the standard brown or blue khaki pants and shirts, that all the other kids wore. Back then, my friends would press a crease in their khakis so tight and with so much starch that those pants could stand up in the corner by themselves.

For reasons that boggled my mind, my mother would send me to school dressed in three-piece suits made of purple crushed velvet, paired with a ruffled shirt and a

2

floppy bow tie. Girls? Forget about it. I couldn't catch a cold dressed like this, and worse, all the tough kids thought I must be rich or something. The result is that I got my natural-born rear end whipped every single day—on the way to school, at school, and coming home, too.

But as I began to wear those suits—as they became my uniform—I started to see suits everywhere. I could now relate to the businessmen who wore suits on television, to the leaders in church who wore suits on Sunday morning, and to my dad, who owned his own business. In time, I started to see myself differently, too. I thought of myself as a businessman.

One day George got shot, just like his role model, Tweet. A straight-A student, George was murdered on a lonely street corner in Compton because he made a decision to hang out with, and look like, a thug—and, I believe to this day, because he did not think for himself. George had all the basic ingredients to become a success in life and a contributor to society, but at age eighteen, because of his choices, George's story was over.

I was determined not to make that mistake. That year, at age ten, I opened my own candy business out of the den of my house—putting the corner store out of that business in the process, because my store was closer to the route kids took to school. (Location, location, location.) I started down a path of entrepreneurship I remain on today.

But more important, I began to learn to think for myself—a skill that would prove difficult to master. I learned

3

that people who think for themselves are much less likely to fall victim to the likes of Tweet or other predatory forces.

In the poor neighborhood where I was raised, like in so many communities in the country, petty thugs preyed on individuals, but white-collar criminals in fancy suits also preyed on poor people's ignorance. Individuals with a low level of basic financial knowledge were and continue to be easy targets for what I call *bad capitalism*.

For example, during the recent subprime lending boom, poor people making $25,000 a year were lured by unscrupulous brokers and lenders into taking out $500,000 loans with low initial teaser rates that reset much higher to levels they could never afford. At one point, my own family lost its home to a predatory lender.

In inner cities today, you'll often find a liquor store right next to a check casher, next to a pawn shop, next to a rent-to-own store, next to a payday lender. If misery loves company, then this is a pile-on. There's simply a super-abundance of predatory businesses, and many people have lost hope. They are poor in spirit: they're not skeptical—they're cynical; they have low self-esteem and negative role models; their get-up-and-go has got up and went. So they go to the check-cashing service to forfeit their today, and go to the payday lender to forfeit their tomorrow. And because they don't believe they'll have a tomorrow, they go to the liquor store to forget about their yesterday.

In these communities, poor people spend roughly $10 billion each year on what I call *ghettoized financial services*—high-interest and high-fee check cashing, payday loans, refund anticipation loans, title lending, rent-to-own, and the like. I know of one individual who got a payday loan for $800; by the time he finished paying it off six years later, after rolling this payday loan over countless times, he had paid $15,000 in interest on that $800 loan. These businesses are in many cases short-term-oriented, purely transactional business models that add little value, and even deteriorate the customer base they purport to serve.

These businesses are ultimately led by one thing: fear. People are afraid to lift themselves up, to lead themselves out of their situation, to think for themselves. Bad capitalism preys mercilessly on these fears.

Throughout my journey from the inner city to my work as a social entrepreneur, I've had a front-row seat for witnessing how fear destroys a community. But I would learn that there is another way to live and to do business. It would take almost thirty years for me to understand that the antidote to fear is love.

## DISCOVERING LOVE LEADERSHIP

In September 2007, I had come to Dalian, China, for the annual meeting of the "new champions," a generation of companies—primarily from rapidly growing emerging markets—that will fundamentally change the global competitive landscape. The meeting was sponsored by the World Economic Forum, an international organization committed to improving the state of the world, which is best known for its meeting of major global leaders in Davos, Switzerland.

I arrived in Dalian four days early to meet with my fellow members of the Forum of Young Global Leaders, the subset of the World Economic Forum composed of more than eight hundred young leaders in their forties or younger who are recognized as rising stars in business, politics, and society. We were grappling with what made us different from others at the forum and what our purpose was.

It was just after the Young Global Leaders (YGL) meeting that I entered the mammoth new glass-and-steel conference center, which had been built specifically for the World Economic Forum's meeting on top of a landfill in what had previously been a poor neighborhood. At that moment, I realized that what set the YGLs apart from most leaders I've met was exactly how we solved problems. It was suddenly so obvious. We did it with *love leadership*.

My friends in YGL, more than any other people I've met, know that there are only two basic ways to lead, because there are only two primal forces in the human psyche: love and fear. What you don't love, you fear. They know that the main reason the world is screwed up now is that most of the world's leaders have been leading with fear.

When many leaders attend a major business gathering around the world, their typical approach is to cocoon themselves. They may arrive in a private plane, step into a private car, drive to a luxury hotel, ensconce themselves in a suite while they study position papers, and then give a speech at the adjacent conference center the next day. They talk about people they have never met, about cultures they do not truly comprehend, and about problems they do not share. And then they wonder why nothing good comes from it, or why the business never truly takes root.

By contrast, when the YGLs arrive for a meeting, we typically load onto a bus and drive often unpaved roads through the countryside to a school or community center, where we talk with kids and other local people. After a few hours of this, we get a real sense of the pulse of that community and, most of all, the needs, wants, and aspirations of the people who live there.

We try to give local people not just the hope of upward mobility—and the strategies that can make it happen—but also something more precious: dignity. We approach them as equals. We build bridges of understanding, and we build relationships, so that when we give talks about some of these amazing people later, we *know* something about them.

The YGLs are also there to do business and help the people they meet do business. What we're doing is R&D. We go, in part, to understand the marketplace, so that we can better *serve* the marketplace. We hope that we can build something together that will last. At the end of the day, we're doing well by doing good. Visits like these are also the emotional highlight of our trip. We leave feeling that we have a real relationship with that community. That we "get it." Working this way also just flat-out makes you a more well rounded and interesting person, which makes you more attractive and valuable in your business and personal life. All in all, it's *good* selfishness.

Back in a meeting room at the Dalian conference center after one of these trips, I sat down at a table and drew a line down the middle of a piece of paper, creating the first, crude diagram of love leadership. On one side of the line, I wrote LOVE. On the other, FEAR. Then I began to list the leadership qualities that characterized each, and the clash of these two cultures became instantly clear.

As I did this, it was as if a dark fog of confusion lifted from me. Somehow for the first time in my career, I felt complete. I found something I had been searching for for thirty years.

Here is part of what I wrote:

| Love | Fear |
|---|---|
| Inspiration | Coercion |
| We | Me |
| Empowerment | Repression |
| Inclusion | Exclusion |
| True wealth | Materialism |
| Forgiveness | Anger |
| Opportunity | Entitlement |
| Spirituality | Nonbelief |
| Ethical questioning | Cynicism |
| Accountability | Irresponsibility |

| | |
|---|---|
| Idealism | Expediency |
| Creating a bigger world | Taking a bigger share |
| Open hand | Closed fist |
| What you're for | What you're against |
| Compassion | Coldness |
| Serving | Self-serving |
| Lifting with love | Failing with fear |
| Empathy | Sympathy |

I gradually became aware that two of my best YGL friends, Shai Agassi and Zainab Salbi, were standing over me. They are both extraordinary. Shai is passionate about using technology to solve terrible social problems. Zainab had grown up in Iraq, where her father had been forced to be Saddam Hussein's personal pilot. She'd been spied on and persecuted by Saddam, and some people had then persecuted her for knowing Saddam. But she had transformed her pain into the creation of one of the world's most prominent organizations that protects oppressed women around the world, Women for Women International. She has shared her story in a compelling memoir, and has been featured on *Oprah* six times.

I showed them what I had just scribbled down.

Zainab stared at the list for some time. "You need to share this," she said. "It applies to everyone. CEOs. Secretaries. Presidents. Parents. Generals. Laborers. Children. Husbands. *This is how people need to treat one another.*" She looked me in the eye, and when Zainab looks you in the eye, you don't look away.

"Write a book," said Shai, simply.

They sat down with me, and we began to refine the list. This was the moment when the formalized philosophy of love leadership was born.

## LOVE LEADERSHIP DEFINED

This book, *Love Leadership*, makes the case, as unlikely as it sounds, that the best way to get ahead is to figure out what you have to give to a world seemingly obsessed with only one question: What do I get?

Love leadership recognizes that you want to do well in life, but it also suggests that the best way to do well and to achieve true wealth over the long term is to do good. I've learned that you'll never go bad doing good, and you'll never be wrong doing right.

*do good*

Love, in the context of love leadership, is not the same as love for your life partner, love for your children, or even love for a big dish of chocolate ice cream. No, I refer to the *agape* definition of love found so frequently in the Bible: love meaning unconditional love for your neighbor, a love as powerful as humankind's love for God. It means treating others as you want to be treated.

Can there really be a place for something as seemingly warm and fuzzy as love in the hard-nosed, eat-nails-for-breakfast, fear-based world of business? As I'll argue again and again in this book, love not only has a place in business but also is absolutely central to sustainable success.

Love leadership is a way of thinking and acting that acknowledges your selfish longings for success and outside acknowledgment, yet also taps the often hidden strength inherent in your personal insecurities, your limitations, even your failings. It mines the wisdom to be found in life's setbacks.

Specifically, *Love Leadership* distills what I have learned about leading, particularly in these turbulent times, into five fundamental laws:

**Loss Creates Leaders.** There can be no rainbow without a storm. That is, there can be no strength or inner growth without the pain of legitimate suffering. Most great leaders came to the wisdom to lead through the endurance of life's trials.

*wisdom*
*endurance*
*of*
*setbacks/*
*trials*

**Fear Fails.** Fear-based leadership rules today's business landscape. But leading through fear is increasingly antiquated and self-defeating. It's a crippling indulgence that we can no longer afford.

**Love Makes Money.** Love is central to success in business. In fact, the expression of love in business—that is, creating long-term relationships with your customers, employees, and community based on caring for others and doing good—makes you wealthy.

**Vulnerability Is Power.** When you open up, people open up to you. Vulnerability is the door to your heart. It grants great power to those who are strong enough to leave that door open. Real leaders understand that vulnerability is not a weakness; in fact, it can be your greatest strength.

**Giving Is Getting.** Leaders give—followers take. The more you offer to others, the more they will want to stay with you, share with you, protect you, and support you. Giving inspires loyalty, attracts good people, confers peace of mind, and lies at the core of true wealth.

*offer to others*

## THE LESSONS OF LOVE LEADERS

I've spent my life studying the rare echelon of people who have gained the gifts of money and power through optimism and trust, and have then used these gifts from the world with the utmost wisdom.

These people, many of whom I'm now blessed to call my friends, are people of great achievement and true wealth. Uniformly, they are fearless men and women. They do not fear the loss of their money, power, or glory—and that's why they have these things.

Some of them have names you most likely already know: former president Bill Clinton, leadership expert Bill George, civil rights leader and former UN ambassador Andrew Young, entertainment entrepreneur and icon Quincy Jones. Others may not be household names, but they should be: HRH Crown Prince Haakon Magnus of Norway, future leader of one of the world's most prosperous nations; Dorothy I. Height, a civil rights pioneer who has advised every president since FDR; and Young Global Leader Darys Estrella Mordan, CEO of Bolsa de Valores, the Dominican Republic's capital markets exchange and the first woman ever to have held such a position in Latin America, among others.

Each of these profoundly important people has created new worlds within his or her own realm, and has found a new way. The exemplary leadership they practice each day has the power to save the world. They are all leaders whose successes have come from caring more about others than themselves. Their power comes from love. That's why people *want* to follow them.

Some have shared their fortunes with the organizations I've been involved with. Even more, though, they have shared their wisdom. They have shown me how the world works, and once you know that, you don't need much else.

## LOVE LEADERSHIP IN PRACTICE

Inspired by the work and lessons of these leaders, I founded Operation HOPE—America's first nonprofit social investment banking organization—immediately following the worst urban riot in U.S. history, as the fires were still smoldering in South Central Los Angeles. There is no better personal and professional example of loss creating leaders than that, as I'll explain later in the book. Starting with one employee, a first-year budget of $61,000, and a vision to eradicate poverty as we know it today, we have now raised more than $500 million to empower the poor.

HOPE converts check-cashing customers into banking customers, renters into home owners, small business dreamers into small business owners and entrepreneurs, and minimum-wage workers into living-wage workers with new job skills. We move people up and out of poverty and onto America's payrolls and tax rolls. We help people help themselves.

Through our financial literacy and economic empowerment work, we show people that the bad capitalism they've experienced is rooted in fear, and that the enemy of fear is thinking for yourself. Operation HOPE operates nine HOPE Banking Centers, a cross between a bank branch and a Kinko's for economic empowerment, offering one-stop shopping for changing your life. When clients walk into a HOPE Center, they are greeted with a sign on the wall that reads "No Loan Denied." We banish fear and give them their dignity back.

Our work on behalf of the poor has been rewarded with long-term relationships with four hundred of the largest banks and corporations in America and around the world, including Citigroup, Wells Fargo, Bank of America, Deutsche Bank, the New York Stock Exchange, and Toyota—even during the worst of the recent economic maelstrom. These difficult times have tested our organization, and many times it has been only my ability to show vulnerability to my board, our partners, and to those we work with that has ensured that our deep connections have endured.

Our work is multiplying with the economic crisis that has gripped the world since 2008. Sometimes we have succeeded in helping clients restructure a bad mortgage to a good one, sometimes we have succeeded in being a compassionate listening ear, and sometimes we have just succeeded in trying.

One story from this work shows how giving really is getting. A Los Angeles family sought our assistance with a $374,000 mortgage and a floating interest rate of 6.5 percent that was due to reset to an unaffordable 8.4 percent and beyond. With the help of Anne-Marie Molina, a HOPE mortgage officer at the Southgate Union Bank of California and HOPE Banking Center, the family now has a 4.5 percent, fixed-rate mortgage. This reduced rate will allow Michael and Galathia to make reasonable payments within their means, live with dignity and hope, and take care of their responsibilities. Their bank gets something in return: a paying customer rather than a foreclosed home.

Together HOPE and its partners are leading what we call the *silver rights movement,* or a movement to make free enterprise and capitalism finally work for the poor. It is a movement that builds on the necessary successes of the civil rights movement, but that also offers the poor and the underserved a practical hand up—not just a handout. The way we serve others is, by necessity and practice, grounded in dignity. Our organization is love leadership in action.

## A PERSONAL STORY OF LOVE LEADERSHIP

Love leadership can work at multiple levels—from the organization, in the case of Operation HOPE, all the way down to the most personal and individual circumstances.

During a visit years ago to Anacostia, across the river and just outside Washington, D.C., I spoke at a public housing project. Even though I grew up in the inner city, the young black men I spoke with that day only saw the suit I was wearing, and they assumed I did not relate to their pain. They sat and listened with their heads leaned to the side and their arms folded.

After it was all over, I was exhausted from the experience, and left for another meeting and then for a late dinner at the Mayflower Hotel in downtown Washington. As I walked into the lobby of the hotel, I discovered that I did not have my briefcase with me. Then it dawned on me: I had left it at the housing project.

I assumed the worst. Here was a briefcase with a White House seal embossed on its side, packed with electronic gadgets and important documents. And I just knew it was gone.

I grabbed a yellow notepad where attendees to our meeting that morning at the housing project had signed in with their contact details. I selected a number at random and called it. A rough-voiced man named Antwon answered on the other end, and I explained sheepishly why I was calling.

"Yeah," he responded, "we got your bag, man. Where do you want us to bring it to you at?"

I was stunned into silence. I offered to send someone to get it from him. He insisted he bring it to me. I gave him the address of the hotel.

For two hours, I waited. Finally, Antwon came strolling through the front door of the gilded lobby. I looked through the briefcase; not a paper was out of place. I had assumed the worst of this community—my community—and they had, thank goodness, disproved my low expectations.

I also found out why Antwon was so late. You see, in all of his thirty-plus years on the planet, he had never *once* traveled across the Anacostia River into Washington, D.C. He had never *once* been in a hotel. As we sat down to have dinner together, I learned that he had never eaten a steak before either, and we made sure he ordered one for dinner with us that evening.

As Antwon left, I asked him what I could do to say thank you. He told me that when I came to speak with him and his crew earlier that day, they did not want to believe what I had to say, because they did not want to be disappointed. They had been let down so many times before by big words accompanied by little action or follow-through.

Antwon told me that before I arrived, he had imagined Anacostia as a community with a chest-high chain-link fence surrounding it. He could not escape. But after listening to me, he said he saw a hole in that fence, and "he was

**17**

breaking for that hole." Bringing me that briefcase was the excuse he needed, the courage he needed, to leave Anacostia for the first time and to cross that river.

Antwon wanted nothing else, he said. He had his payment.

I was not tired anymore.

Oddly enough, it was a briefcase and a dream that ultimately saved both Antwon and me.

While we were having dinner, my chief of government affairs, Jena Roscoe, arranged for Antwon and his wife to go to a special engagement at the Kennedy Center the next evening. They would sit in the box reserved for the president of the United States of America.

This is what having power is all about—giving it away. Giving Antwon this gift was pure selfishness for me, and it felt good. My story of loss and my sense of vulnerability made a connection with this young man, and that helped him banish his fear and change his life, and ultimately his economic situation, for the better.

## WHAT LOVE LEADERSHIP OFFERS YOU

This book is about hard-nosed leadership in the twenty-first century. It's simply a new approach to leadership, one that allows you to strive as hard as the next person and achieve as much as you are humanly capable of. But it is a uniquely humane brand of leadership that lets you sleep well at night, too, one that reminds you that your life has purpose and meaning, and that even as you receive you have something valuable to offer this world. Love leadership offers a legacy that you can truly be proud of.

A core part of *Love Leadership* is based on my life's experiences and lessons, which are interspersed with stories and lessons from the leaders who've taught me what leading with love is all about. As I tell my story, I will strive to paint an honest picture of my personal, community, and business journey. I won't sugarcoat the truth: for every stirring success, there was a crushing failure. That's life.

This is my story of leading with love, of overcoming my own fears and insecurities, of healing my pain, of living a life I can feel reasonably proud of—and of *doing well for myself*, too. It is also a story about the power of love leadership—to transform business and the world.

I hope that there is something here for you.

# 1
# LOSS CREATES LEADERS

Loss is personal for me. I learned the importance of the first law of love leadership—loss creates leaders—when I was a child and my family struggled with money problems. It was my family's collective loss that led me to become the leader I am today.

The number one reason why families divorce in America is money, and this sad fact became a reality in my home when I was five. Up to that point, my family had been living the American dream. Here was a hard-working, enterprising black family from the South, headed by a mother and father armed only with an eighth-grade education. (My mother would go back to school at age sixty-two to receive her high school equivalency, later marching in cap and gown to obtain her diploma in a sea of eighteen-year-olds.) Within a short period of time, my mom and dad accumulated their own home, an eight-unit apartment building that we rented out, a nursery my mother ran, a gas station in South Central L.A., and a construction company my dad ran.

There was only one problem: my dad was financially illiterate, and too proud to admit it. He would make a dollar and spend a dollar and fifty cents. The more money he made, the more broke we got. Just as quickly, we lost almost everything.

The apartment building went, and the nursery went, and the gas station went, and soon my mother went. There were arguments and then a fight that turned physical. At age five, I had to call the police on *both* my parents for beating up on each other. One day, my mother went to the bank to withdraw the $4,000 of life savings she had accumulated to send my brother to college, only to find that it was all gone. My dad had gotten there first. That was the last straw. Messing with my mother was one thing, but messing with her dreams for her children, that was something altogether different.

My dad was and is a great man. I loved, even idolized him. It was not common among his generation to show much emotion or even to say, "I love you," but I knew that he did love me. There's no denying, though, that understanding the unique language of money and how the financial system worked has always been his blind spot. After their divorce, my dad was able to hold on to his construction company, but he would never build any real wealth or assets to speak of.

Around the ninth grade, I moved out of my mother's house in Compton, California, to South Central Los Angeles to live with him. Life with my dad was both easier and harder than living with my mom and sister. There were no bothersome chores, but he compensated for that with an obsession that I get the quality education he never received, that I stay away from girls, and that I work in his construction company when I had extra time.

The Reverend Dr. Martin Luther King Jr. once said that "a man cannot ride your back if you are not bent over." My dad was a proud man, with his back straight up. But one day a mortgage broker showed up at our house and began to sweet-talk my father into a refinance of his home.

Unfortunately, my father was a bit too proud, and he failed to ask critical questions that would have guarded him, and us, against financial predators. And when he did ask questions, they were the wrong ones. My dad asked, "What's the payment?" instead of "What's the interest rate?" As we've seen in the subprime mortgage crisis, when low teaser interest rates later exploded upward and threw millions out of their homes, you should never ask what the payment is when an interest rate is attached.

My father signed what is known in the predatory lending business as "a perfect eyesight loan": twenty points and 20 percent interest. You get the loan, and you go blind. When the rate resets upward automatically after a short

23

time, you can't afford the mortgage, and the lender fore-closes on your house.

In the end, we lost our family home in just this way.

## MY FALL FROM GRACE

I got my work ethic from my dad, but I learned *financial literacy* from my mother. She worked for many years and retired from McDonnell Douglas, now Boeing. In addition to working at her job, she often sold things to her cowork-ers, from candy (wonder where I got that idea from?) to a range of handicraft and food products that she would sew and cook herself. This augmented her income and pro-vided her a measure of independence as well.

My mother learned from the loss and the lean years of her childhood, first in Carbon Hill, Alabama, where she and her sisters grew up in a shotgun shack, and then later in East St. Louis, where her parents moved for a better life. When she was a little girl, she would work outside the house to make money for the family: scrubbing floors on her knees and digging up roots to sell to make wild-crafted medicines. Her dad had died when she was very young, leaving her mom to raise six children alone.

I recently asked my mom how she became financially literate. She told me:

I had worked all day and my mother would say, "Baby, you got any money?" She loved to play the numbers and play the horses. But I always had the sense to never tell her how much I actually had. If I had $4, I'd tell her I had $2.

"Let me have it," she would say. "I have a feeling I'm going to be lucky today. I'll pay you back."

And I'd give her the money, and the next day would be the same. And so I learned that charity starts at home. If I was ever going to have anything, I had to make sure I saved something for me and my future, even while I was trying to help my mother and to contribute. I had to accept that while my mother was amazing on many levels, she was not perfect.

I admire her for what she did—she built a house in East St. Louis for $500 in cash money she had saved. In spite of her being a gambler, she still taught me the value of money. I took the bad and made good out of it. I remember saying to God when I was seven years old that if I ever got to be a grown woman and had any children, I hoped I would raise them better than I was being raised.

She vowed never to be poor as an adult. Her children would have the financial resources and the love that they needed to live a dignified life. And we did. She went on to buy and sell five homes, and today she is financially independent, living in Houston, Texas.

My mother understood that life wasn't about making more money; it was about making better decisions with the money you made. When she said she was going to purchase a car, she meant in cash. The entrepreneur in her would often tell me growing up, "The man will set your salary, but you decide your income."

Despite her teachings and my desire for a different financial life than my father's, I ultimately ended up in a similar spot and for similar reasons: losing the roof over my head because I couldn't manage my money. This is how it happened.

When I was about fifteen, I told my dad I wanted to go to private school. My father didn't want to admit that he didn't know how to *get* me into such a school, so he just said, "You find the school, and I'll pay for it."

Being only fifteen, I had no idea how to choose a school. So I took out the phone book, opened it up to private schools, and ran my finger down the listings until I reached the Hollywood Professional School. After the success of my candy business, I knew I wanted to be a businessman. "Professional school" sounded like a business school to me.

When I arrived at the school for a tour, I kept passing all these famous child actors: Todd Bridges, Tatum O'Neal, Griffin O'Neal. I finally realized I was in a school for child actors, not a business school. The Hollywood Professional School held classes in the mornings for kids in the entertainment industry who were actively working. These actors didn't want to go to school on the set. They wanted a normal life and to be around other kids in entertainment.

At my interview, the ninety-year-old director of the school stared at me for the longest time, trying to figure out which TV show I was on. But it was impolite to admit you didn't know who someone was in Hollywood, so she just assumed I was somebody. I didn't exactly lead her to believe otherwise, so she signed me up for school, and my dad wrote the check.

Casting directors naturally found the school to be a convenient one-stop shop for child actors. I got my first few minor acting gigs just from sitting in the classroom as casting directors would come in and announce, "Who's interested in the next show?" I began to get some bit parts on a number of TV shows, eventually landing minor roles on everything from the hit show *Diff'rent Strokes* to an episode of *The Twilight Zone* starring actor Danny Kaye. One thing led to another, and I became a child actor myself.

I was what I call an illegitimate child celebrity. By that I mean I was acting, but my promotion of myself as an actor was far better than my acting itself. This was when I began to appreciate my talent for marketing, but admittedly, my product was still weak. Nonetheless, by the time

I was seventeen, at the height of my acting career (such as it was) I was bringing in thousands of dollars every week. The problem was, I was spending a whole lot more than I was making. I had the lifestyle to match: I lived in a beach house in Malibu with Kevin Wilson, comedian Flip Wilson's son. Eddie Van Halen lived nearby and would come over for our wild parties.

Around that time, I decided I wanted to become an entrepreneur. I started one money-losing business after another. Every entrepreneur wants to be shot out of a cannon, including myself, so it was a bit of "ready, fire, aim." I had the ambition, but I was impatient. I lost my shirt over and over again. If I had any redeeming quality at the time, it was that I never, ever gave up.

The last straw was a concert promotion business I ran when I was eighteen years old. I was promoting a concert for one of the many former lead singers of the Platters, and the concert was a first-class flop. That was the end-game for me. At that point, I ran out of options.

I went from living in a beach house in Malibu to living in my black Montero Jeep near the airport. I parked my Jeep in a desolate parking lot behind an old Italian restaurant at the corner of La Tierra and Airport Boulevard in Los Angeles, where no one would notice me. Just to be sure, I put my car cover over the Jeep and then dropped it over the back door as I crawled inside for the night. I kept food in an Igloo.

Oddly enough, whenever I get driven to the airport these days, now by a car service and not in an old Jeep, I pass by the location where I was homeless all those years ago. Every week I am reminded of where I could end up if I were to make those same stupid mistakes again. You never get too big for your britches.

My dad lost his house and much of his wealth because he didn't know enough about managing his money. In contrast, I knew better: my mother taught me valuable lessons about making a living. I wanted to avoid my father's financial mistakes, but I was young and full of pride, not paying attention to both making and keeping my money, and I landed right where he had.

## LEADING FROM LOSS

I regularly meet with executives of powerful companies in my work on behalf of Operation HOPE. People sometimes ask me how I deal with the ever-present possibility of rejection from these high-powered CEOs. I say, "What are they going to tell me, 'no'? I've been homeless for six months. I've been on the floor of life, and you can't fall from the floor. What is 'no' after that?"

I lost almost everything when I was homeless. But the interesting thing is that once you understand what loss really is, once you lose someone dear to you, or once you lose yourself, you gain the world.

Once you learn that the world didn't come to an end and that you could work your way back to being whole again, you gain enormous confidence and wisdom about how to live: how to have humility, what matters and what doesn't, how to succeed against all odds. It builds up an enormous strength inside you.

Most people find strength in things that are outside them: money, power, titles, wardrobes, cars. But most of the things that make a leader are on the inside: integrity, wisdom, confidence, vulnerability, joy, passion, compassion, intuition. These things come from life experience, from life's trials, from the deepest part of a person's soul. You can't fake them, and you can't buy what's not for sale.

My mentor Rev. Murray says, "Life asks a question of every leader that gauges their effectiveness and wisdom: 'What have you been through?' Following battle, King Arthur would have his knights line up before him, asking of each, 'Show me your scars.' If none existed, he would say to the warrior, 'Leave me and go get your scars.'"

I have learned that authenticity counts, and that the best route to an authentic life is through your scars. As you earn them, you learn to drop the B.S. in your life and to attach yourself to the substance in your life—and to the substance in those around you. Precisely because of that history of loss, you never take yourself too seriously or get needlessly seduced by short-term materialism. In other words, loss helps ground you as a person.

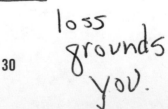

There's a hard lesson in life's setbacks: *just as steel is forged through fire, leaders are forged through loss.* There can be no strength, no real inner growth, without the pain of legitimate suffering. It's a scientific fact: you cannot have a rainbow without a storm.

That's why I believe that the first law of love leadership is that loss creates leaders. If love leadership means learning to think clearly for yourself, putting others first, and banishing fear, it is loss that lays the groundwork for the kind of growth that leads to a love-leadership perspective.

Loss creates leaders with a competitive advantage earned in the school of hard knocks. The advantage comes from the tremendous personal and professional growth loss generates. And rarely does that growth lead in directions you could or would have predicted.

The storms of life offer an opportunity to respond in one of three ways to personal tragedy or failure:

1. You can give up.

2. You can try to cope using whatever dulls the pain most, be it alcohol, drugs, sex, work, money, or success.

3. You can grow and create something useful out of your experience of loss.

The choice lies between legitimate suffering now and illegitimate suffering later. The first two options are what I call *illegitimate suffering*. Giving up and coping are code

31

words for avoidance, and the story of avoidance never ends well.

Only the last option allows you to harness fear and turn it into the strength to lead with love. The route to real growth is through legitimate suffering. Managing your personal sense of loss gets you there strongest, fastest, first.

Loss is wisdom acquired early.

Wisdom comes from dealing with your mess. All of it. But few people want to do that because it is just too much: too much work, too much acknowledgment, too much remembering, too much pain. But I have found that there is freedom in surrendering to this work, to saying "Yes, that happened, but it doesn't define me. What does not kill me will only make me stronger. I made a mistake, but I am not a mistake."

*I am not a mistake*

The net effect of saying this over and over again in your life, of reaching a wall and climbing over it, is increased confidence in yourself, and faith in others and this world of ours. As strange as it sounds, loss is making you stronger, with every round.

The calmest place is the eye of a hurricane, but most people in their fear would almost instinctively flee to the edges of the hurricane instead. What if we all made a commitment to live centered in the storm? After a while, we'd get used to the center of the storm. Storms would not seem so bad after all.

Now all of this may sound brave, and maybe even courageous, but it is not. What we call courage is nothing *an act of faith*

more than an act of faith, of reaching through fear. We display this quality publicly to others as what we call "courage." Ask people who have done something deemed courageous, and they will tell you they did not feel courageous at all when they did it. They felt scared, just as you and I would in that situation. What made the difference was how they responded to their fear.

*purpose — comfortable in your own skin.*

I believe that the whole purpose of life is to become comfortable in your own skin. How do you do that? Simple. Learn to get out of your own way. How often? Every single day.

You are the best asset and absolute worse obstacle in your life. No one can help you better than you, and no one can hurt you more perfectly. No one in this world knows you better.

Becoming comfortable in your own skin comes from dealing with your pain, from getting on the other side of fear, from experiencing loss and appreciating its inherent lessons of wisdom and learning—and all the while *discounting* its ultimate long-term value in determining your outcome in life.

Becoming reasonably comfortable in your own skin is the goal, and experiencing, managing, and surviving personal loss is the all-time best route.

It has worked wonders for me. Every time I walk into the office of a Fortune 500 CEO or a world head of state, I remember that I was homeless and survived it. After that moment, I am free and easy. So, too, will you be.

## GREAT LEADERS FORGED BY FIRE

Most great leaders in the world have come to the wisdom to lead through loss.

Franklin Delano Roosevelt contracted polio when he was thirty-nine years old. He persevered and became president for four terms, leading America out of the Depression and to victory against fascism. Rainbows after storms.

It was the loss of her thirteen-year-old daughter to a drunk driver that led Candice Lightner to found Mothers Against Drunk Driving (MADD), which has saved the lives of thousands of people. This work has likely helped her put her own life back together as well. Rainbows after storms.

Banker Leslie Maasdorp lost his freedom to South Africa's vicious apartheid regime. He had risen up through the ranks as a student leader and was thrown in prison for thirteen months. He remembers:

> The irony of the prison experience is that it was actually one of the best things in many respects. For the first six months when I was detained I had no books. And then the university fought a case against the government, and the high court decided students who were registered before they were arrested must be allowed to continue their studies. So I had my books again. I was in a single prison cell, alone, and I received my degree cum

laude. As a result of receiving my degree cum
laude, I got scholarships anywhere.

He went on to earn a master's degree in economics from
the University of London, then moved back to South Africa
after apartheid ended. He worked in the African National
Congress government for seven years, first as an adviser to
the minister of labor and later as the deputy director general in charge of restructuring and privatizing state-owned
enterprises. In 2002, he was recruited to work as an international adviser for Goldman Sachs. Today he is vice chairman
of ABSA, the largest retail bank in South Africa, which is
owned by Barclays Capital. Rainbows after storms.

At age eighteen, Rodrigo Hübner Mendes was studying to enter the medical school in São Paulo, Brazil, when
he was shot through the neck in a random, senseless
carjacking.

He remembers seeing images of his young life flash
before his eyes, but suddenly having a sensation that his
story was not over, that he had to finish his story: "And at
that moment, I just said, 'No, I will not die.' And when I
said no, I just came back to reality, to real time, and I was
lying on the floor. After you pass through this point where
you get very close to the limit, to the extreme, that shows
you other perspectives. It changes your point of view."

Mendes began a slow rehabilitation to recover some
movement, but remains in a wheelchair and paralyzed
from the neck down. One day during his recovery he met

*extremes*
*&*
*changed*
*point*
*of*
*view*

an artist who offered to give him painting lessons. Mendes began to produce series of watercolors. Soon his work had garnered enough acclaim to call for a public exhibition.

In 1994, he founded the Rodrigo Mendes Institute, a visual art school dedicated to creating opportunities for low-income minorities and people with disabilities in Brazil. Mendes later went on to business school and launched a career as a consultant at Accenture, the global Fortune 500 consulting firm, overcoming his disabilities to lead a team of consultants and gain the respect of the executives he worked with.

After four years, however, Mendes faced a choice: continue at Accenture or go back to leading his art school. He remembers:

> I compared the two options I had. If I decided to go on as a manager at Accenture and if I was successful, what would be left of my story after my death? "Rodrigo became an executive; he was successful; he overcame his disability." That's OK, but compared to the second option, which would be to help Brazil improve its education model and to offer opportunities for an important portion of the population, that would make me much more happy. Nowadays the Institute maintains projects in different states of Brazil offering training to public schools regarding inclusive education.

My experiences showed me that happiness is a point of view. Happiness is not a result of what you conquer compared to what society believes; happiness has to do with how you see the world and the point of view you follow during life.

*Happiness*

We have a strong power to define the size of our challenges or, if you wish, of our adversities. When I am dealing with some obstacles, some kind of difficulty, I always try to remember that I have this power to minimize them and to make the best of any kind of situation. If you take a look at the life story of any kind of human being, you will see that there are a lot of things that happen with us that we are not able to control. Normally we don't see these changes and these surprises as sources of opportunities. Since we are not prepared, most of the time we don't take advantage of them, and we just lose opportunities to grow.

*power to define the size*

For my political hero, former president Bill Clinton, I believe that his point of view was changed radically after both public and private losses in his life, including, of course, the well-publicized scandals and his impeachment and later acquittal. Here is a man who is clearly stronger and, it appears, even wiser following the setbacks in his public and private life. If it weren't for the storms of his presidency, I am convinced that the world would not have had the benefit of the full focus of one of the most brilliant political minds and most authentic public servants on the planet.

Clinton told me recently that the defeats in his life, including his earliest political setbacks, have only made him stronger:

> When I was young, I often lost [student] elections in part because I was in the band and not a star athlete. Then when I didn't come out on top in music contests, losing was even more painful. My mother taught me not to feel sorry for myself and told me to keep trying. She said I had good health, a good mind, and good friends, so I should just count my blessings and do more with them.

> When I was defeated for reelection as governor in 1980, I was in bad shape and full of regret that I would no longer be able to do the work I loved so much. At that moment, there didn't seem to be much future for me in politics. I was the first Arkansas governor in a quarter of a century denied a second two-year term, and probably the youngest ex-governor in American history. But if I hadn't been defeated, I probably never would have become president. It was a near-death experience,

but an invaluable one, forcing me to be more sensitive and understand that if people think you've stopped listening, you're sunk.

Out of his loss has come extraordinary global leadership. Since leaving office, his work—from the Clinton Global Initiative, to the various initiatives of the Clinton Foundation, to his work with Operation HOPE to help over a hundred thousand survivors of Hurricane Katrina—has impacted millions around the world. I am convinced that the best is yet to come for him.

Another one of my heroes, Quincy Jones, told me that loss makes some people swing for the fences the next time, to put even more at risk. He learned that lesson after he recovered from being in a coma and had two surgeries for a life-threatening congenital weakness in the arteries of his brain:

> As you go through life and as you stumble, psychologically you retreat. And you become cautious and reticent and a little careful about things. So a simple victory encourages you to make a giant step the next time and another giant step. As soon as you fall you get right back up and hit it again, and you make giant steps. And then you get to the point where nothing scares you, which is where I'm at now.

You try and try again and put more at risk, which puts you in an even greater position to succeed. I'll put it even more succinctly: success means going from failure to failure without a loss of enthusiasm. You just never, *ever* give up.

Dr. King gave his "I Have a Dream" speech a hundred times before the historic march on Washington in 1963. An instructor at Crozer Theological Seminary gave him a C+ in public speaking and said that if King didn't stop speaking the way he did, he would end up an utter failure.

But King had passion, and he decided to continue to be the individual he was. He didn't give up on the fiftieth speech when kids were going to sleep in the church, or the eighty-fifth speech when people were walking out the back door. If he had given up the ninety-ninth time, America would be a different place today. But he gave that hundredth speech, and you know what? America finally believed in his multicolored dream. As a result, there is a man named Barack Obama who is the forty-fourth president of the United States of America today.

Dr. King never gave up, even when he faced death. Civil rights leader Andrew Young, King's top lieutenant, told me a little-known story about the time in 1960 when Dr. King came face-to-face with the possibility of the loss of his own life:

Martin was arrested for picketing at the Atlanta sit-in, and they took him to the Fulton County Jail and charged him with violating probation for driving in

**40**

Georgia with an expired Alabama driver's license. They put him in chains on his hands and legs, chains behind him, and threw him in the back of a paddy wagon with a snarling police dog.

He was rolling around on the floor in chains, and they drove him from Atlanta to Reidsville State Prison, which is over two hundred miles away on bad Georgia roads. It was an eight-hour ride with death.

He very seldom talked about that experience. He laughed and joked about being stabbed, and he talked about his home being bombed. Everything else he could deal with comfortably. But that was the time he came to grips with death. And he used to say, "You say you're ready to die—you just don't know. But once you cope with that fear of death, you don't have to fear nothing else."

That's how loss creates leaders. Loss strips away your physical crutches, and even your emotional crutches, and leaves you with nothing but the spirit. And in the spirit lies your true power.

Loss fires your spirit, and it steels your mettle. Even if the hardship you've experienced in your life is more prosaic than Dr. King's, you have experienced your own personal pain: the loss of a job, a personal betrayal, a major disappointment. And out of that pain, you gain not only strength and a competitive advantage but also something even more essential: learning. Learning is the source of your advantage.

Not many people know that California banking leader William A. Hanna, managing director with California Technology Ventures and the Jacobs Capital Group, flunked out of McGill University. He went back and graduated in the top third of his class.

Then he almost flunked out of Harvard Business School. At the end of the first semester, he got a call from the dean threatening to kick him out of Harvard if he didn't shape up. Hanna committed himself to spending the next three months in the library, and earned his MBA. He learned something from these experiences that stuck with him:

> Those defeats and setbacks have come because I was not focused and because I was not committed. I did not know what I was getting myself into, and I did not get into the details enough. When you focus, when you're committed, when you get into the details, and when you have the support from your family, there's nothing that can stop you from succeeding. Absolutely nothing.

*focus*

Crushing defeat hits hard because you never want to admit that you failed. I ran Bank Audi California with Joe Jacobs, and Joe used to have a little sign on his desk that said, "Babe Ruth struck out 1,330 times." We don't think about Babe Ruth striking out 1,330 times. We just think about him having 600 home runs. But the fact is, he struck out a lot.

## LOSS GIVES YOU AN ADVANTAGE

"At the end of the day, we're dealt the cards we're dealt to make us stronger," my friend Lynn Pike, president of Capital One Bank, told me recently.

The cards I've been dealt—my family's collective loss due to divorce and money problems and my own personal business failings—have not only made me stronger but also made me the leader I am today, working to fight the very banking practices my family fell victim to. Not only that, my loss gives me a competitive advantage.

I say this humbly, but without flinching: you can't compete with me in my space, because you can't compete with passion. Most employees show up nine to five. They're very nice people, but they're passionate about their family, and they're passionate about their hobbies. I go from six in the morning until nine at night every day. My people are on fire with changing the world and eradicating poverty.

It's just like the magic of compounding interest— except I've got the magic of compounded hustle, and I'll run circles around most people because I'm passionate. Financial literacy is personal to me. I will put things at risk that most people wouldn't.

*passion*

43

That perspective comes from loss, and in particular from my experience with homelessness. The personal story I shared with you at the beginning of this chapter was not complete. See, I wasn't completely destitute when I was living in my car: I had $500 a month coming in from the residual payments of various acting jobs. At that moment, however, I faced a choice—rent an apartment, which was socially acceptable, or rent an office, which might make me some money. I decided to rent an office on the border of Beverly Hills from a friend who had extra space in her public relations firm's office suite. I would stay there late in the evening working on marketing for a few small-business clients until everyone left, when I could use the twelve-by-twelve-inch restroom sink to wash up. I had to leave the office about midnight for my Jeep, or else the security guard would start to become suspicious.

Even though I was technically homeless, I always made sure I had on shiny shoes and a clean white shirt. I would scrimp a couple of bucks to get my shirt cleaned, or even clean it myself in that tiny sink. I knew that people noticed those touches as a sign of professionalism. I kept up this routine for six months, when I managed to pull myself out of my predicament.

I finally got myself out of that Jeep thanks to the help of Dave O'Meara, who owned Malibu Cinemas at the time. One evening after I had worked a full day at my office, I went to see O'Meara around midnight in his office. (OK, it was the candy and popcorn counter at Malibu Cinema.) I asked him to invest in yet another wide-eyed business idea.

He told me, "Look, I believe in you, John, but about the only way you're going to give me my original money back is if you get a job somewhere." I had never had a job, so he asked his friend Stephen Cotter Miller of Wade, Cotter, and Co., a private merchant banking company in West L.A., to take a chance on me.

I had no experience in banking whatsoever. Wade, Cotter wanted me to do equity loans. I said, "That's great. What's an equity loan?"

I didn't realize it meant lending money to poor people in the inner city who couldn't afford to pay it back— exactly the kind of predatory lending that claimed our family home. As far as these bankers were concerned, they were providing a straightforward service. But to me there were morals and ethics involved.

So I said, "I know people in Hollywood who can afford to pay your money back. When they work they have significant income, and they have assets you can loan against in the short term. Why don't you let me show you how to make some real money?"

I brashly convinced my boss to create a new lending division and put me in charge as a partner. He wouldn't have to pay me a salary, I proposed, just straight commission. I even agreed to share whatever profit I made 50-50. I think he said yes just to shut me up.

My first year, I failed the California real estate test that I needed to pass to do home lending—three times, which is very difficult to do. If you can breathe on a mirror and walk straight, you can pass this test. I didn't. I also made zero in revenue my first year, and everyone in the office laughed at me behind my back.

The second year, I finally passed the test on the fourth try. I brought in $9 million in transactional revenue. The third year, I brought in $15 million; my fourth year, $24 million. No one was laughing anymore.

When the company I worked for ran into financial trouble in 1991, I bought out my division and started the Bryant Group Companies. I did some loan servicing, some investing, some merchant banking. And with all that going on, I was still bored.

I remember asking God, "What's my purpose here?" And sometimes you have to be careful asking questions like that, because God may actually answer you.

## OUT OF LOSS AND DESPAIR, HOPE

On April 29, 1992, I got my answer. I was looking out the floor-to-ceiling glass window on the eighth floor of my Westside offices, trying to figure out my purpose in life. On that day, the Rodney King trial was just ending. I thought the L.A. police officers who had been videotaped viciously beating King after a high-speed chase would surely go to jail for what they had done, just as King would surely go to jail for stupidly running away from them.

And then the trial of the police officers who beat King ended—all not guilty. And it destroyed my world. I was angry, frustrated, disgusted. I wasn't alone. Later that night, I turned to look out the south-facing window of my office in West L.A., and all of South Central was on fire. The police and firefighters retreated and just let the neighborhood I grew up in burn down. And it broke my heart.

The first thing I could think to do was to go down to my church. The First AME Church was where all the power brokers were meeting during the crisis, and that's where the spirit of bipartisanship was born in me. I sat with my spiritual father, the Reverend Murray, pastor of First AME Church then, who had raised me as much as my parents had. He was the person who held his hands out and kept Los Angeles together when even ten thousand law enforcement officers and the National Guard couldn't. A pastor with the voice of moral authority, compassion, and fairness held L.A. together.

In his office, I quietly sat in the corner as a student and just observed. And there was Governor Pete Wilson, a conservative Republican; there was Mayor Tom Bradley, a moderate Democrat; there was Rev. Jesse Jackson, a fiery liberal advocate. And they were all talking, to *each other*. There were conservative, buttoned-down CEOs in the room, too, and they were all asking the same questions:

"How do we move forward? How do we get Los Angeles working again?"

That was when I decided I wasn't a member of the Republican Party or the Democratic Party. I was a member of the Get It Done Party. I vowed at that point that I would talk to anyone who had solutions for my community. I didn't really care whether you were black or white, rich or poor, conservative or liberal, Republican or Democrat: if you wanted to help me eradicate poverty in my community, you were my friend. If you didn't, you were just wasting my time.

I stopped Rev. Murray, who was very busy, and I said, "What can I do to help? I'm not a politician; I'm not a community leader. I am a businessman. I am a capitalist with a heart. What can I do?"

"John, you wrap all these people up together, and all you have is a potential bus accident," he said. "These folks cannot rebuild a community. *You* can rebuild a community. God made you for this moment. Take your business skills and put them to use."

It was first-rate advice. I took it, all the way down to the part about the bus—except that this one wasn't about to get into any accidents. This bus was headed straight for South Central with people aboard who had the connections and money to rebuild.

I left Rev. Murray's office, called some folks, and told them I was going to organize a Bankers Bus Tour. It dawned on me that people were watching L.A. burn on

CNN as if Beirut were on fire thousands of miles away. I knew that this kind of disconnection and indifference was the death knell of the soul.

I also knew, from practical experience in the banking industry, that you don't lend where you've never been. Bankers would prefer a 7 percent return on the Westside over an 11 percent return in South Central, because all they saw of South Central on TV was crime, mayhem, and brutality.

I understood what many lenders didn't see at the time: if you drove down the commercial thoroughfares, it might look like a war zone, but if you took a right turn down a residential street, you might as well have been in Ozzie and Harrietville. Residents had the pride of home ownership.

So I took the spiritual realm of the Reverend Murray, the advocacy realm of the community leader, the business realm of the banker, and the bipartisan realm of effective politics, and put them all together and created Operation HOPE as a partnership between government, the community, and the private sector. We would be the glue that brought everything together for poor communities who lacked banking services; who lacked financial literacy; who lacked a path to home ownership; who lacked a path to economic self-sufficiency; who lacked dignity, power, or even the simple courtesy of a returned telephone call.

The riots started on April 29, and by May 4, South Central was still burning. But on May 5, it was calm enough for us to organize what became the first of our many Bankers Bus Tours.

I remember Bernie Parks, then deputy chief of police who went on to become chief of police of Los Angeles and now a prominent councilman, saying to me, "You want to put white folks on a bus and drive them *where*?"

"I'm doing it," I said.

"Well, hold on, let me send you some police," Parks said.

I can still see the scene vividly: we had eighteen bank CEOs in a motorbus, and police units drove on all sides of us with shotguns aimed out the window as we drove through South Central L.A.

As we were driving, I got up at the front of the bus as if we were on a tour at Disneyland, and I started telling the CEOs the story of the buildings and the communities they were passing through. I gave them a sense of history and dignity about these neighborhoods they had never thought about or been to.

I told them that three thousand structures had been damaged in the riots, at a cost of about $5 billion. Then I asked how many homes they estimated were destroyed. And the bankers threw out estimates as high as 10 percent.

"Wrong," I said. "Zero. Actually, one home technically burned down, and it burned accidentally because it was structurally connected to a commercial building."

Rev. Murray is the best commonsense economist I know, and he says, "You don't burn that which is your own." People burned the commercial buildings that belonged to absentee owners who funneled money out of the community, but they didn't burn their own homes.

At the time, black people owned only 35 percent of the homes in South Central. African Americans rented the other 65 percent for the same cost as a mortgage payment. And I told these bankers they were looking at a market opportunity. If people are renting for the same cost as a mortgage payment, wouldn't they prefer to own? And wouldn't it be in America's best interest for them to own?

Here's the magic, though. If 35 percent home ownership gave the community the perception that African Americans owned all the real estate, and thus it wasn't touched, that gave me an enormous degree of hope. You didn't need a majority for a tipping point. You only needed to reach a certain point and then the community's spirits would tip toward hope.

If bankers would offer people responsible, consistent payments at a fixed rate that was equal to or lower than their rental payments, which the bankers could easily afford to do at the time because interest rates were low, then residents could build equity for their family and pay their property taxes. The bankers did, and both they and the community benefited. This was responsible lending, and everyone won.

Continuing on the tour, we came across a man named Gil Mathieu at 42nd and Western streets. He owned a pharmacy that had burned down. We stopped and the bankers got out. Mathieu explained that he couldn't get a loan from the Small Business Administration to rebuild his pharmacy because it wanted three year's worth of tax returns. Of course, his tax returns had burned in the building. And I got out a brown paper bag that was in the bus, tore off one side of it, and said, "Who's in?" A little bidding war broke out right there on the sidewalk for a piece of Mathieu's loan.

Let me be clear: not one of these bankers was willing to fund this man's $400,000 loan and rebuild this pharmacy by himself. They thought it was too risky. But together, eight institutions combined their resources, lowered the perception of risk, and funded that loan. Mathieu eventually used only $100,000 of it, financing the rest out of his cash flow and giving back the remainder of the money. And he paid off the loan within a year. Handler's Pharmacy is thriving today.

That was the beginning of Operation HOPE. No one can solve the problems of poor communities by themselves. The banking industry is looking for markets, communities are looking to become stakeholders, governments are looking to create a tax base. That's enlightened self-interest, a central tenet of the Operation HOPE plan.

I saw the inner cities as an emerging market, and the Bankers Bus Tours were like trade missions to a developing country. And pretty soon we went from one Bankers Bus Tour with eighteen people to ten chartered buses, seven hundred bankers, several high-level cabinet members, government officials, and the chairman of the FDIC. And in the sixteen years we've been doing this, we've never had a single act of violence or an accident with anyone on a

Bankers Bus Tour. In fact, after seventeen years we have never had even one incident at any of our HOPE Banking Centers in inner cities across the nation. And we are in the *money business*, in the "hood."

I learned through this experience of loss that <u>people didn't want to tear up their communities</u>. I was just as frustrated with the outcome of the Rodney King trial as people in South Central were. But Operation HOPE decided to handle that frustration in a different way. Some people responded out of fear, frustration, and a lack of hope. We responded with <u>love and patience, empathy instead of sympathy, the long view.</u> We believed that this community offered a way for the business community to do well and to do good, too.

Operation HOPE was a way for me to do well and do good, as well. Ultimately, this work has saved me—from myself. If it hadn't been for the work of Operation HOPE over all these years, I'm sure I would have been obnoxious, self-absorbed, and very wealthy, but lonely. Giving other people dignity gave *me* dignity.

Loss has saved me.

And it is saving others. We have served over a million people to date.

We're changing the face of poverty. And all because I experienced loss. Loss really does create leaders. It puts you on the path toward love leadership—leadership based on the <u>strength born of struggle.</u>

*leadership born of struggle.*

And you'll need every bit of that strength to banish the fear you face every day in business.

# 2
# FEAR FAILS

As a leader, I'm *far* from perfect. There have been plenty of times in my career when I have allowed my lack of self-awareness and my hard-charging energy to bring down the people around me. And every time that has happened, it is because of fear: fear of myself, fear of imperfection, fear of failing.

And what I've learned time and time again is that fear doesn't work. In the long term, letting fear motivate your actions—how you treat others, how you conduct business, how you live your life—leads to failure.

The second law of love leadership—fear fails—can be explained best in terms of where fear comes from and where it leads.

Fear is a lazy bastard. It comes from the most primitive part of what evolutionary psychologists call the reptilian brain, the part of the brain that governs instincts,

*no work*
*no intelligence*

heartbeat, and breathing. It takes no work and no intelligence. Even a lizard can be afraid.

Love, though, comes from the most advanced part of the mammalian brain—the forebrain—the region that thinks, remembers, and finds meaning. Fear is a feeling and nothing more. Love, in contrast, is feeling *plus* thought. It's an emotion that stays in your memory forever. That's why love survives, long after fear dies. Love is so strong that it's the only real reason the human race is still here, after all the opportunities we've had to destroy ourselves.

## A FEAR-BASED WORLD

Álvaro Rodríguez Arregui is a Young Global Leader of the World Economic Forum and the cofounder and managing partner of Ignia, an investment firm based in Monterrey, Mexico, focused on commercial enterprises serving the poor. He thinks fear lies behind the two major motivators that he sees too much of in major corporations around the world: ego and greed.

> I think that ego and greed both boil down, in the final analysis, to fear. They're fear disguised by two of its many faces. And in business, fear is the kiss of death.
>
> If you have a job in a big corporation, you have to walk through that door every day thinking that this

may be your last day on the job. That's just modern corporate reality. But if you go through that door with fear, it will be your last day on the job. Because if you give in to fear, you won't create, you won't take responsible risks, you won't innovate, and you won't make space for new talent. All you'll do is cover your ass. And you will not achieve anything meaningful.

Fear too often stems from low self-esteem as well. Former president Bill Clinton told me:

People fear failure, inadequacy, rejection, a recurrence of past hurts for themselves or loved ones, and the unknown. No one is immune to some or all of these fears. That's why real living takes courage—to act, grow, change, and get up and try again and again.

A lot of powerful people in this world, oddly enough, have a poor image of themselves. Outwardly, low self-esteem manifests itself in arrogance, in a sort of brutality in the way leaders manage. Business for them is a zero-sum, winner-takes-all competition.

Self-esteem is critical to combating fear. I learned early in my life that if I don't like me, I cannot like you. If I don't learn to love me, I cannot love you. If I don't respect me, I won't respect you. And here is the biggest lesson: if *purpose!*

I don't have a purpose in my life, I am going to make your life a living hell.

Charity begins at home. You've got to feel good about yourself before you can feel good about anything else. You'll fail in life if you don't have self-confidence. You'll fail even more spectacularly if you lack what leadership expert Bill George calls a True North—if you don't have a purpose in your life, if you don't believe in something larger and more important than yourself.

*larger than yourself*

Says civil rights leader Andrew Young:

What is it that people fear? People fear themselves. You have to love yourself and know that God loves you as you are. And what is it that most of us fear? Most of us fear rejection. We fear the emptiness and anxiety in our lives, and so we're always looking for affirmation, understanding, acceptance from others.

*from within*

But it can't come that way. It has to come from within, when you're no longer afraid of who you are. It's like President Roosevelt's statement, "The only thing we have to fear is fear itself." While he was applying that to the nation and the world, the truth of it is that each person every morning has to wake up and say, "I'm not afraid to face this day. I am up to the task, whatever it might be."

If you believe, in essence, that you're God, that nothing exists beyond you, that you're the be-all, end-all of the universe, you're a very dangerous person. You can rationalize anything. And to rationalize is to tell rational lies.

There is an old Southern phrase, "No matter how much I love you, my son or my daughter, if I don't have wisdom, I can only give you my own ignorance. I can only give you what I have got." Because we don't know better, we don't do better. Oddly enough, out of a sense of uninformed love, we pass down our bad habits from generation to generation. Fear begets fear.

Why do we let fear drive us? Fear causes us to lose control of our lives little by little. We start out in life with a little fear, and we try to kill it with a little money and power. And the next thing we know we're getting old and we have a *lot* of fear, and we try to kill it with a *lot* of money and power.

When we look for love in all the wrong places, all we find is fear.

## FEAR-BASED LEADERSHIP

Look around you in the corridors of business today, from the biggest corporation to the tiniest mom-and-pop operation, and you'll see a picture of fear just as vivid as some of the streets in the inner city where I grew up. Everywhere around us we see seemingly successful leaders who practice what I call *fear-based leadership*.

Henry Ford II was a classic fear-based leader. His executives learned they had been fired when they came to the office one day and found that their furniture had been removed from their office, or sometimes chopped to bits and left in a pile in the center of the room along with their personal belongings. Employees lived in mortal fear of that fate befalling them.

The dot-com stock market meltdown of the early 2000s felled a great number of leaders from companies built on fear and greed. Once-invincible firms with multibillion-dollar valuations, such as Enron and WorldCom, are now extinct. Once-lionized leaders—Bernard Ebbers, Jeffrey Skilling, Dennis Kozlowski, and the like—are serving long prison sentences for fraud.

Not much has changed lately. These days, Scott Rudin holds the ignoble title of "most feared boss"—he's a "Boss-Zilla," according to a recent article in the *Wall Street Journal*.[1] Rudin is a Hollywood film producer who is responsible for a string of hit movies, including *The Hours*, *The Truman Show*, *The Royal Tenenbaums*, *The Queen*, *No Country for Old Men*, and *There Will Be Blood*. These successful films have reportedly come at a high personal cost to those around him, however.

Rudin fired 250 assistants over a five-year period, and he has on occasion fired his entire staff all at once, according to news reports. One assistant was allegedly fired for bringing him the wrong muffin. Rubin is well known for being foulmouthed and throwing things at his assistants.

It's said that some of his assistants have measured the length of the cord on his office telephone, so as to stay out of its reach when he throws it at them. (Things allegedly got worse when he acquired a Blackberry.) One assistant said, "His business is one that operates out of fear."

Rudin was voted New York's Worst Boss by the readers of Gawker.com,[2] and was featured prominently in the best-selling book *The No Asshole Rule*, by Stanford professor Robert Sutton. He is reported to be the model for the evil film producer that Kevin Spacey played in the 1994 film *Swimming with Sharks*.[3]

Rudin is not alone in using fear to intimidate those who work for him: in one large survey, 37 percent of American workers reported being bullied at work.[4] One in six workers in a 2000 study reported persistent psychological abuse.[5] Bosses are the main culprit.

Fear-based leadership tactics include the following:

- Using aggressive language, tone, and eye contact
- Criticizing unfairly
- Blaming, without offering reasonable recourse
- Applying rules inconsistently
- Stealing credit
- Making unreasonable demands
- Issuing threats, insults, and accusations
- Denying accomplishments

- Excluding others from opportunities

- Assigning pointless tasks

- Personalizing problems

- Breaching confidentiality

- Spreading rumors

Lynn Pike has seen the damage that such tactics can cause in the workplace. Today she is president of the banking division of Capital One, and she has more than thirty years of banking and community development experience at Bank of America, FleetBoston, and Wells Fargo Bank.

*someone else's fault*

When people lead from the perspective of fear, they can be intimidating. They're not open. They don't listen. They're not willing to admit when they've made a mistake. It's always someone else's fault.

That kind of leadership model is not sustainable. It might produce decent performance over a short period of time. But I don't think you're a leader when you lead through fear—you're a manager.

Pike has witnessed the transformation of team members who have left a fear-based environment and come into the environment she creates, one that's open and safe, where you're allowed to be yourself and have a point of view and take risks, where you're encouraged to learn from your failures because—guess what?—failure is good.

"What happens is you have a team that is more centered, committed, and willing to take the hill," she says. "You've got a team that can overcome adversity because they're a lot more resilient. People are lining up to be on your team because it feels like it's a more empowering and vibrant place. It just makes you feel good."

To use fear is a leadership choice that goes back centuries. In his famous sixteenth-century treatise on power, *The Prince*, Niccolò Machiavelli asked whether it is better for leaders to be loved or feared:

> The answer is that one would like to be both, but since it is difficult to combine the two it is much safer to be feared than loved, if one of the two has to make way. For generally speaking, one can say the following about men: they are ungrateful, inconsistent, feigners, and dissimulators, avoiders of danger, eager for gain, and whilst it profits them they are all yours. . . . Men are less worried about harming someone who makes himself loved than someone who makes himself feared, for love is held by a chain of obligation which, since men are bad, is broken at every opportunity for personal gain. Fear, on the other hand, is maintained by a dread of punishment that will never desert you.[6]

Machiavelli, it turns out, was dead wrong. I saw fear every day on the streets of L.A., and it was *always* a one-way ticket to failure, or worse. That's why I say, in the second law of love leadership, that fear fails.

Look at such leaders as Gandhi, Rev. Dr. Martin Luther King, the Dalai Lama, Nelson Mandela, Franklin D. Roosevelt, Mother Teresa, César Chávez, Abraham Lincoln, and Jesus. Compare them to Joseph Stalin, Adolf Hitler, Osama bin Laden, and other fear-driven leaders.

One type of leader chose to light a candle; the other chose to curse the darkness. Both types of leaders were undeniably intelligent and charismatic, and even had a vision for the future. Both succeeded in getting the masses to follow them with that vision. And the choices of both types of leaders had momentous outcomes that have defined generations to come.

But only one choice is the right one, and only one choice leads to success over the long term.

## FEAR LEADS TO "SHORT-TERMISM"

The problem is that the entire business world seems to have come down with a case of attention deficit disorder. The disease goes by another name: *short-termism*. Short-termism is similar to fear and laziness, in that it relies on shortcuts to achieve results.

For most people looking for a short-term fix, fear-based leadership wins out, hands down. If you're satisfied

64

with flash-in-the-pan, short-term thinking, there's no better way than to lead based on fear. With luck, your business will take off like a rocket for a while. Eventually, however, it will implode.

Says Frank Krings, chief operating officer of Hypo Real Estate Holding and formerly Deutsche Bank's COO Europe:

> You may create short-term focus by using fear. And that may work for a couple of hours or a couple of days, maybe for a couple of years. In the short term it may work, but there's no way that fear leads to any sustainable result in the long run.

One of the most significant examples of the failure of fear-based leadership motivated by the desire for a short-term fix or shortcut is the subprime mortgage crisis that has gripped the capital markets the world over. Huge losses on foreclosed homes have morphed into a full-blown credit crisis, a liquidity crisis, and ultimately a crisis of confidence that at the time this book was going to press rivaled the Great Depression in its severity.

Neighborhoods have become awash in foreclosure signs. Layoffs have rippled through companies of every size. Ordinary people have found it hard to get the credit they need to run their businesses and their households.

The root of the crisis lay in a toxic combination of fear, greed, and laziness. And it emerged from the bedrock of American wealth: housing. Everyone in the mortgage industry was trying to get rich quick while the sun shined. No one cared what happened if home owners couldn't repay their mortgages. Everyone was busy cutting the biggest slice of the pie—for themselves.

While housing prices rose, home owners "made money" refinancing their houses to buy things they couldn't afford, pushing up household debt to a record 133 percent of disposable personal income by the end of 2007. Brokers and lenders made money available to anyone who wanted a loan, welcoming speculators and those with no ability to repay. Investment banks made money repackaging home loans into complicated and opaque new securities. And money managers and insurance companies made money borrowing staggering sums to buy and insure those securities. Of course, all that money has now evaporated—the ultimate form of failure.

The financial industry was structured according to the theory that if risk could be dispersed widely, losses from any future disaster would be spread out to so many unrelated entities that it would not crush any one of them. That was the theory, but not the reality, as Wall Street learned.

In fact, few of these cheerleaders of fear, greed, and laziness actually cared about the risks they were taking. Even people in charge of risk management were caught up in the game. One employee who rated mortgage-backed securities was caught e-mailing his colleague, "We rate every deal. It could be structured by cows and we would rate it."[7]

When you don't understand what you're buying and don't care what you're selling, the whole game can unravel as quickly as a Ponzi scheme. Wall Street normally runs on equal parts fear and greed. Now fear alone rules.

But short-term-minded fear can be defeated, as we'll see in the next chapter, through the power of love for the long term. But first I want to show you how, as a leader, I've allowed myself to operate from fear, and later learned to put that fear aside.

## STUMBLING AND FALLING, OUT OF FEAR

I remember back in 2000 when Operation HOPE was planning our first-ever national inner-city economic summit. We were under enormous pressure to pull it off. Back then I would make commitments to do things, not recognizing that everyone on my team had different priorities and that they thought and did things differently than I did.

I had written a letter to Al Gore, who was still vice president of the United States at the time and was soon going to be running for president. I told him that I wanted to start a network of inner-city cybercafes. I asked for his help, and in the process asked if he would keynote our economic summit.

The way I write is to headline my vision. I say, "I'm going to do this." But when Gore read the letter, he interpreted it to mean that we had already built the cybercafes. He wrote back saying he loved the idea and that he would be in Los Angeles in two weeks to tour our inner-city cybercafes, and while he was there, he would speak at our summit.

The only problem was that there were no inner-city cybercafes. They were merely an idea. But when I called his office to try to find another date, his staff said, "You are the last thing on the vice president's schedule in his official capacity as vice president. After this, it's all campaign events. It's this or nothing."

So I went down to our HOPE Center in South Central L.A., and I stood there with Fred Smith, a dear friend of mine who still works for Operation HOPE today. I put out my thumb, aimed it right down the center of the building, and said, "Fred, bulldoze the right side and turn it into a cybercafe."

"What do you mean?" he said.

"The vice president's coming here in two weeks," I said. "I promised him a cybercafe. The Bible says, 'Where there is no vision, the people perish.' We're going to create a cybercafe."

"With what money? With what energy? With what time?" he said. "You can't build something in two weeks."

"Never say *can't* and never say *impossible*," I said. "Just start bulldozing. I'll figure out the rest."

Fred started bulldozing. I went back to my office, called a senior official in the Department of Commerce and said, "The vice president of the United States is coming to South Central L.A. to visit our cybercafe."

"Great," he said.

"The problem is, we don't have a cybercafe," I said.

"Oh, no," he said. "What do you need?"

I said we needed $400,000 to build the cafe, and that if he would match half, I would raise the other half. It was the fastest federal grant the Commerce Department had ever processed. I didn't have anyone to match it, so I then asked the White House for the name of its top outside technology expert. White House aides gave me the name of Steve Ryan, an attorney who at that time was with the Manatt, Phelps & Philips law firm.

I called Steve Ryan out of the blue, and he wasn't impressed. I was fast talking, and I told him what I wanted to do. He said, "You're nuts. You can't do this in two weeks."

"Never say *can't* and never say *impossible*," I said. "The difficult you do immediately; the impossible takes a little longer. I'm told you can do the impossible."

"Tell me your vision," he said. I told him my vision, and he said, "Meet me in New York in two days."

I flew to New York, and sat down with him and his wife and had cocktails. We talked about generalities and for five minutes about my vision for the cybercafe. I left, thinking it was an odd meeting.

The next day Ryan called me. "I'll help you," he said. He said his wife was an excellent judge of character, and I had passed the test.

I told him I needed $200,000, but he said he didn't have access to anywhere near that amount at the time. Then I said, "Look, there are two ways to make money: you make more or you spend less. If you can't help me make more, help me spend less. The $200,000 breaks down as follows: wood, lumber, computers, software."

He told me he couldn't help with the wood or the lumber, but that he could help with everything else. Meanwhile I went to Hilton Smith, corporate VP for community affairs at the Turner Construction Company, and got a commitment of $40,000 in wood and lumber. Then I went back to Steve Ryan, and he put together a conference call with his technology network. After a rocky start, most of the people on the call started to pipe up with offers to provide the software and the computers. Then I went back to Smith at Turner Construction and asked if he could start construction immediately. Smith said no.

"The vice president of the United States is going to be in our community in eight days, and we don't want to be embarrassed, do we?" I said. "You can tell your grandchildren for the rest of your life that you helped build the cybercafe in South Central L.A."

So the contractors showed up and did the work for free. And we nailed the last nail into the last beam on midnight before the vice president's visit. It was a great day for South Central L.A. and for our community. And that cybercafe has now served hundreds of thousands of people.

Although the cybercafe was a success, at times my leadership performance was less than stellar. The events leading up to the construction of our cybercafe were the hectic backdrop for our economic summit. I was going a million miles an hour. At that point, the summit wasn't coming together the way I had wanted it to. It takes about twelve months to design a professional summit for a head of state. We were doing it in two weeks. And I was under a tremendous amount of stress from building the cybercafe.

But it was *my* stress. It wasn't the stress of anyone on my staff or our volunteers. It was my drama, and I was dumping my drama on everyone else.

One day I just snapped. It was ten at night, with a week to go before the summit. Things weren't coming together as fast as I wanted and the way I wanted. The actual incident involved something as trivial as the printing of a program.

I stood on my desk and screamed at the top of my lungs, "What the hell are you guys doing? Are you out of your goddamn minds? The vice president's showing up. I want this done!"

And everyone around me was just shell shocked. Rod McGrew, our first volunteer at Operation HOPE, in particular should have walked out. He had been donating his time every week for eight years, and for the previous two weeks on the economic summit. There isn't a week that's

71

gone by that Rod hasn't selflessly given his time as a volunteer—advising me, serving on the board, volunteering in the classroom, helping out my staff with strategic planning. He wasn't being paid, and while we were preparing for the summit, he was working until ten at night instead of being with his family. He should have said, "I'm out of here. You're out of your mind."

But I've learned that in life people will forgive you every other sin as long as you're authentic. Rod knew that I was being authentic, even though I had an incredibly bad bedside manner and was enormously insecure. He knew I was under a huge amount of stress, so he forgave me.

"Look, I'm going to forgive you that tirade, but don't do it again," he said. "Now, what do you want me to do?" And then we finished our work for the night.

It was fully within his right to curse me out, but he didn't use that power. He chose to be gracious. He chose to be kind. He chose to use the experience as a lesson, through his own action, of how someone could handle a situation in a different way and yield a better outcome.

Fear had me in its grip, but with those calm words, fear let go. Rod's love and grace under pressure taught me a tough lesson that day. From then on, I would not let fear control me. I would tame my fears and push through them, with dignity for myself and those around me.

Mentors in life like Rod have taught me that when you really have the power, you don't need to use it. I would learn to talk without being offensive, to listen without being defensive, and to leave even my adversaries with their dignity. I would learn to love those I did not like. I would love those who did not deserve love in return. Then and only then would I be totally free.

It takes the power of love to banish fear. As we'll see next, love leadership puts love into action. That love takes the form of long-term business relationships built on caring and doing good—like those with Rod and others whom I've been lucky enough to learn from throughout my career. That kind of love leads to its own reward.

# 3
# LOVE MAKES MONEY

Growing up, I tried almost every conceivable way to make money. I wanted to get rich, and I was in a big hurry to do it. In my teens, I launched an automotive detailing business and a mail-order business and several other enterprises that died in rapid succession.

When I was eighteen, I started a concert promotions company and almost lost everything. At my first concert at a new convention hall in Rialto, California, there were more folks on my payroll than individuals in the audience. My so-called friends whom I had hired to help stood in line to be paid at the end of the night, even though it was obvious that the venture was a first-class flop. I learned that night that I needed a completely new business strategy, and maybe some new friends, too.

One day while I was still living out of my Jeep, I decided to start a business that wholesaled Fila and Ellesse sportswear. Back when I was growing up in the 1980s, everyone wanted to wear Fila and Ellesse clothing. It was the "in" thing to be in. I wanted to wear it too, but not only did I not want to pay for the clothes, I wanted someone to pay *me*.

The people I knew in the neighborhood were buying knockoff goods that looked like the real thing but were manufactured fraudulently. The fraud thing was just not for me. I didn't want to go to jail, I didn't want to wear fake goods, and I didn't like the way I felt when I did something wrong, yet alone illegal.

Being completely vain, I wanted to wear the real thing, but could not afford the $100 to $1,000 price tag that real Fila and Ellesse goods commanded at the time. As I researched the brands, I discovered they had divisions in Mexico. I could drive my beat-up car from Los Angeles across the border and purchase legitimate Fila and Ellesse products at a fraction of the U.S. retail price. A business was born—I thought.

Soon I began bringing in sportswear from Mexico by the trunkload, and made a 100 percent profit selling items to my customers in the United States at half the usual price. In this early venture, I was smart about generating a profit, but I did not have enough common sense to keep the enterprise relatively low key. I saw no reason to hide what I was doing. After all, I thought, the goods were legitimate.

For a teenager, I was making a lot of money, and I got loud and overly confident about my newfound success.

Over time, I have always found this combination to be a warning sign of impending failure.

I rented a modest but well-located showroom space on the west side of Los Angeles, and then I actually went into legitimate Fila and Ellesse outlets and encouraged them to buy from me and not their corporate parents. It was breathtakingly bold.

It wasn't long before the companies' investigators paid me a visit. I wasn't hard to find—after all, I had given the outlets my business card printed with my name, phone number, and address. The investigators assumed I was simpleminded and that I was also trading in counterfeit goods, like everyone else. They purchased a couple of items from my store, leaving puzzled when they saw that the goods were real.

In the end, Fila and Ellesse sued me for unfair competition. When I asked my attorney what this meant, he said simply, "You broke no laws, per se. Frankly, John, you outsmarted them. This lawsuit is simply their way of putting you out of business by drowning you in costly legal proceedings. Walk away from this and feel good that you are smart enough to make it." I did, and I did.

From that moment on, I knew I could become a success in this world: I had applied myself, crafted a business plan, created a value proposition, started a new business with little capital, worked hard, and made money. But I also recognized that I didn't want to make money just any old way.

It had to be honorable. I began to understand, through my own mistakes, that there was a difference between good capitalism and bad capitalism. I wanted to do well for myself, make no mistake about it, but I also wanted to find a way to serve society, not just serve myself and get paid.

As I would eventually learn, doing well by doing good is the essence of the third law of love leadership: love makes money.

## LOVE-BASED PROSPERITY

There are only two things in this world: love and fear. What you don't love, you fear. In my teens, I was running my early businesses out of fear. As we've seen, fear is me-focused. It is short term. It is based in greed.

When I was running these businesses, I was hustling without a larger purpose beyond my own selfishness. I was thinking about the short-term buck, but not the long-term business. What I was doing wasn't illegal, but it was unethical. Sure, I was hurting Fila and Ellesse's bottom line, but it was dangerous to my well-being as well. The erosion of a person's character often occurs little by little over time, and it's but a slippery slope from rationalizing bad behavior to committing bad deeds.

The alternative is love-based *prosperity*. What do I mean by that? The third law of love leadership—love makes money—breaks down into a set of interlocking and related goals: *creating long-term relationships built on caring for others and in service of a larger good.* Each goal is guided by love. When you operate this way, the by-product can't help but be prosperity for everyone, which naturally leads to money for you, too.

That's because love always leads to money. Money is nothing more than one of the many by-products of love leadership. That's right: money, over the long term, is simply another confirmation that you're doing good work. It's a by-product. It's never *the* product.

No entrepreneur worth his salt—and I think of game-changers like Bill Gates, Ted Turner, Richard Branson, and many others—ever started a business just because he or she wanted to make billions of dollars. These people probably didn't mind the idea of making a lot of money, but they started in business because they were obsessed with an idea. They were *idealists,* in the broadest sense of the word.

Gates was obsessed with the idea of empowering people with knowledge through easy-to-use software; Turner was obsessed with empowering people with information through a twenty-four-hour news network that would inform the public about events as they happened; and Branson was obsessed with a long list of business innovations, from airlines and cell phone service to space tourism and alternative fuels. Each leader was obsessed with a vision that he had for himself and for the world. And along with being passionate about an idea came the money—but only as a by-product.

Because these entrepreneurs did their work in a way that lifted society—that did well and did good—everyone won. Thanks to their work, all boats rose, and not just the yachts. They were focused on a prosperity agenda for everyone, not a money agenda for themselves.

The third law of love leadership—love makes money—means thinking about others more than you think about yourself. It means *caring* for others: what they think, what they need, what they want. It means not just putting customers first, but also thinking from the customer's point of view—what they think, what they need, what they want. Caring for others means giving a damn about people as people, not as transactions or as means to an end—and not just because it's the right thing to do, but also because it's in your own self-interest.

After all those years of failing at business, I came to realize that the only way I was going to succeed was by building long-term relationships. This law of love leadership means being in business not out of greed, but rather out of this larger purpose of caring for others and doing good.

But caring for others and doing good require taking the long view.

## LEADING WITH LOVE FOR THE LONG TERM

If you want to grow your business wildly over the next few months and meet your profit projections over the next few quarters, there is no more effective way than the fear-based model of leadership we saw in the last chapter. Nothing works better in the short term than intimidating the hell out of people and coercing them to do exactly what you want. They'll jump to attention every time you come into the room, and agree with everything you say.

Of course, you can't be too concerned about your reputation, your brand, your future, your credibility, or the loyalty of the people around you. You just have to bark orders, and hope for the best. This is the playbook of the schoolyard bully.

Over the long term, however, things are different. To simultaneously succeed and to be happy you need to lead with love. Tom McInerney of ING Americas shares a long-term, love-leadership perspective on business. ING Americas provides banking, investments, life insurance, and retirement services for the mass market, so McInerney feels everything his company does is based on the long-term good of society. He says:

> With the growing, expanding middle class, there are great opportunities for businesses to focus on this market segment. For us, we are able to offer financial products and services to make it easier for Americans to plan for retirement. Helping them invest and save allows us to make a positive difference in their lives, empowering them to better manage their financial futures.

Daniel Sachs also understands this crucial difference between fear and love over both the short term and long term. Sachs is CEO of Proventus, a $750 million private investment company in Stockholm, Sweden, that invests internationally in companies in need of change and develops them for the long term. As he explains:

> If you're doing things that in the short term
> are good for you, but in the long term are ruin-
> ing society, you're building a less equal and less
> humane society where prosperity is not widespread.
> You may not have a consumer to sell to in twenty
> years. But if you have a long-term perspective, you
> realize that you cannot build your actions on your
> own short-term interest alone. Everything you do
> for the long-term interest of society is also good for
> your own long-term interest.

Proventus bought a 125-year-old company called BRIO, known around the world for its high-quality wooden toys. The toy business is probably the most globalized industry in the world. Four percent of the world's children live in America, but 45 percent of the global toy market is in the United States, and 90 percent of the toys in the world are made in China. And if you look at a basket of toys made in the last five years, the same toys are 40 percent cheaper now than they were five years ago.

For a mature company with production in Sweden, these facts represented an enormous challenge. The company found it had no choice but to move production to lower-cost countries in Asia. BRIO built a factory in China with a partner, ensuring in the process that it was environmentally sound and that the partner paid workers pensions, created a good work environment, gave workers enough free time, created a council for employee complaints, and granted the freedom to join a union. Continues Sachs:

> If I believe in the principle of what's good for society in the long term is also good for me, then we cannot apply other standards to our manufacturing in China than we would if it was at home. In the short term this makes our costs higher. We could have bought our toys cheaper. But in the long term, we want to build a factory with workers who will learn to build our product well, who will be comfortable and safe, who will have a good enough living standard. That's the foundation for our long-term success.

> It's up to the people who believe in markets and believe in globalization and believe in free trade to make the case for an open society as appealing as we can to the many. Because if it's not good for the many—if it's only good for the few—then it's not going to win. It's up to us who believe in markets and in capitalism to devise a model of capitalism that is more long term.

As Sachs has shown, if you want to be still in charge a year from now—or five, ten, or twenty years from now—you've got to build something that lasts. To perpetuate your power into the future, whether you're growing a business, leading a government, nurturing a family, or running a team, you need to earn the love and respect of those around you, and you need to love and respect them back.

If you lead with love for the long term, people will follow you forever, wherever—for their own good as well as yours—and you will be remembered as a person of greatness.

## CARING FOR OTHERS

We've seen that the key to love leadership is a long-term orientation toward caring for others, but can that really pay off in money?

I learned through trial and error that if I treated my business partners and clients as transactions and not as relationships, I would get that one sale, but not twenty. There would be no customer next year, and my business wouldn't be sustainable. If, in contrast, I treated others the way I wanted to be treated, I learned that they actually wanted to do business with me more, they trusted me more, they were more loyal to me, and they had more confidence in me. Love really does make cold, hard cash, too, but only if you build real relationships with your business partners, customers, employees, coworkers, and stakeholders.

I'll say this simply: long-term relationships based on genuine caring are the financial engine that drives love leadership. That said, the real wealth of these relationships has absolutely nothing to do with money, but rather with the intangible but priceless value of the relationships themselves. At the end of the day, we don't do business with governments or companies or organizations, but with people. How you treat people when times are good and how you treat them when times turn bad will define your true measure of wealth.

Real relationships also take a real investment. If you treat your customer like an object in a transaction, is that work? Probably not. If you take the time and nurture a relationship, is that work? It's a hell of a lot of work. But there's also a huge payoff. You won't get paid one time; you'll get paid several times as that person gives you multiple levels of business. You'll also receive many nonfinancial payoffs that I believe have incalculable value over and above anything monetary.

The basic question is this: Would you prefer to do business with someone you like and trust, or someone you don't like and don't trust? The answer to that question is inherently affirmative, and demonstrates better than words how love, how relationships, always lead to prosperity, and to money, too, if that is your aim.

The problem is, relationship building is often misunderstood as networking. Traditional networking "techniques" and the building of real relationships are radically different activities, however. Networking is a one-way relationship; building relationships is two-way. You will never see Bill Gates, Bill Clinton, Quincy Jones, or Andrew Young at a networking reception.

Americans aren't usually accustomed to building real relationships. It's a cultural thing, says George Haligowski, chairman, CEO, and president of Imperial Capital Bank, which is headquartered in La Jolla, California, and is the seventh-largest chartered financial institution in the state. Haligowski was born and raised in Japan by an American father and a Japanese mother (and is bilingual), and later moved back to the United States, so he has a uniquely Japanese and American perspective on business. He says:

> Japanese business relationships are totally different from the way Americans conduct themselves in business. For example, in Japan it takes a long time before you actually do a transaction with a company. You build a relationship first, and you learn to like each other first before you make a business presentation. I've seen so many occasions where American companies race in to Japan, and they meet the people, they throw out their business cards, and the first thing they want to do is conduct a transaction without a basis of any real human element or relationship existing.

> I have built both my personal life and my business career on the foundation of sustaining lifelong

relationships that go beyond the mere transaction. When you take the time to build relationships with people, they are concerned about you, and you are concerned about them. You are "bound up together in a mutual destiny," as Martin Luther King once said.

When I go into someone's office for a meeting, I always make a beeline for the person's photos and mementos. I am genuinely interested in other people's lives. (I also know that most people are *even more* keenly interested in their own lives.) Sadly, few people they meet ever ask them about their family, their interests, their passions, or what *they* want. Most people walk in with their hand out. They think the meeting is all about the "ask" or the "sale."

In contrast, I look at a meeting as a wonderful opportunity to gain a new friend, colleague, or partner in the world. And that is the differentiating factor between building solid relationships and networking. Networking is about me, not we.

Most folks are defensive in meetings. They start out almost expecting that you are only there to get something from them. That's a horrible way to start a meeting, so I always change the dynamics as soon as I possibly can.

A lot of people are cynical first, and hopeful only with cause. It is the unfortunate legacy of living a life surrounded by takers and salesmen. Whatever the reason for it, you need to get the people you meet off of that notion as soon as possible, for your own good and theirs. Consider yourself an orchestra conductor, able to change the entire shape and tone of the experience with a word or gesture. You will be amazed how much power you have to influence the agenda simply by the way you handle yourself.

By asking the other person about his or her family and children (and who doesn't like talking about their children?) you send a message: I care about you, and I am interested in something beyond what I might get. From there I inquire about the person's hobbies and interests beyond work, and ask my favorite question, "What are you passionate about?"

Because businesspeople rarely get asked about themselves, they generally open up. And since most people's favorite topic is themselves, and their most important word is probably *I* or *me*, once they open up they tend to talk nonstop for twenty minutes about their life, their career, their interests, and their family. That's a good thing for you, for this new relationship, and perhaps especially for the person opening up. People who know that they count and who have a sense that they matter in this world are healthier for it.

After that first question, my favorite thing to say to people I care about and respect is "What can I do to help you?" This really floors people. When was the last time someone asked you what he or she could do for you, and meant it?

Sometimes I will even make my intentions clear by saying, "You can relax. This will be the easiest meeting you will have all day, because I don't want anything from you. No requests. I simply wanted to come and visit with you, share my vision, and, I hope, build a relationship." Ninety-nine percent of the time, that statement does the trick. The other person is now completely relaxed, and maybe even relieved, and best of all I have met a new and valuable friend.

Want to hear something crazy? A big part of my job at the nonprofit I run is fundraising, but I never ask anyone for money for Operation HOPE or any of my initiatives. Of course, at the appropriate time I may send a proposal outlining a pressing need, or mail something to document the substance of what we do, but I never ask. I have raised $500 million this way, by not asking and not selling. I have found it much more powerful to share, but this of course means that you actually have to believe in what you are sharing and doing. You cannot fake authenticity.

I have learned that there are much better ways of selling than selling. What I mean is that if I push myself on you and somehow actually get you to buy something you didn't really want to buy, you are going to experience buyer's remorse. But if I simply share my vision with you, with an eye to somehow enrolling you in that vision, I will get the sale I want—a long-term relationship—and typically much, much more. (Again, this approach does require a sense of passion and authenticity to work, mind you, but so does love leadership.)

I cannot tell you how many times I have gone into a meeting only to hear toward the end a CEO say, "So, what can I do to help you?"

When I came to the office of the CEO of Hawthorne Savings Bank, I thought I was there to try to justify his bank's becoming a new investor in our movement and that this relationship would result in $25,000. Then he asked me, "What would you do with $1 million?" Glad I hadn't asked for anything.

Then there was the time I shared my vision with the then CEO of E*TRADE Bank, Arlen Gelbard. I never mentioned a dollar figure. Today E*TRADE is one of the largest investors in our work, with a $10 million, ten-year commitment that has resulted in the people of Anacostia, outside Washington, D.C., and the people of Harlem, New York, being served with dignity and banking services through Operation HOPE Banking Center in their communities. Even in the midst of the worst economic crisis of our generation, and under fire as a company, E*TRADE has never hesitated in keeping its commitment to me and to HOPE.

In both cases, these leaders ultimately asked me, "What do you need, John?"

That's how we took Citigroup from being a $25,000 donor with eight volunteers in 2002 in Harlem to a multimillion-dollar donor and our first global partner. Citigroup is giving us almost twelve hundred volunteers to support our work today, in locations that range from South Central Los Angeles to South Africa. I don't have to sell Citigroup. Now we've got relationships from the top executives of that organization to middle managers, over to our project managers, and all the way down to the thousands of company volunteers who are singing the praises of Operation HOPE. And these relationships lead to the company's continued financial support.

To makes these ideas more concrete, let me tell you about two companies: Wells Fargo and U.S. Bank. These two stories prove that building long-term relationships based on caring for others does pay off financially in the long term.

## Wells Fargo

Wells Fargo loves its customers. Yes, *loves*.

Wells Fargo is in effect a modern-day community bank with a focus on local bankers serving local communities. It is not a traditional national bank, but rather a series of decentralized regional banking centers within the bank that foster local decision making, manage their own balance sheets, invest back in their local communities, and maintain valuable customer relationships.

In Los Angeles alone, the bank invests up to $12 million every year in the South Central community. It's also the most profitable division within the bank, and those two things are related.

The result of this love leadership is a bank that knows its customers, understands their changing needs, and engages in hands-on customer service. It's not a saint, by any means, but it treats customers extremely well, and that counts for something.

When I call my banker to talk about my checking account and then decide I want to make a change to my home mortgage payment or discuss loan options for a four-unit apartment building I am thinking about building, or if I want to apply for a credit card or line of credit, the same banker handles it. I don't get bounced around from department to department, having to repeat myself five times to five different representatives. My banker brings up all my records on his computer screen. If there is a question he cannot answer, he gets someone else on the telephone with us, and we all sort it out together.

As a result of this superior customer service, the bank has more of my business than it otherwise would have. This $600 billion behemoth actually cares about me, and because of that, it doesn't just have my checking account or my mortgage; it has a substantial part of our family's entire financial world. And because it has taken the time to build relationships, the bank has gathered so much information about customers like me that it is also able to recommend other banking products, such as a college savings account or an IRA, when someone comes in for a mortgage.

Authentically connecting with people and building genuine relationships have the added benefit of translating into increased opportunities and long-term financial gain for all involved. Wells Fargo once again stands out here. In 2003, before the subprime mortgage situation was apparent to most everyone, the bank did something odd. It turned away easy, short-term profits.

Cara Heiden and Mike Heid, copresidents of Wells Fargo Mortgage, knew that love-based relationships took hard work. When subprime mortgage financing was in its heyday, many banks and mortgage companies were offering so-called liar's loans, because customers would state their income and assets without documentation. Loans like these were bringing substantial revenue to the bottom line.

Heiden recalled that time to me recently:

> We believe in doing right by the customer. So when the customer comes to us for financing, we work hard to ensure that they in fact have the ability to repay that mortgage loan, and that we're setting them up for success.

> In the fourth quarter of 2003, we sat around a table and looked each other in the eye and asked, "How do we know that these customers have the ability to repay?" We didn't have the confidence that they did, and so we concluded that it was wrong, and we decided to stop doing stated-income, stated-asset subprime financing.

> We brought the leadership in who were responsible for the subprime sales force. At first, many of them thought we were nuts because we were giving up this revenue. We had sales reps walk out.

Heiden was frequently challenged that she was losing significant market share for the company to more aggressive lenders. And she was: the decision kept Wells Fargo out of roughly half of the subprime market, and it made it more difficult for salespeople to originate loans for new customers, because of the full documentation now required.

Those were lonely days for Heiden and Heid, and in the short term Wells Fargo's business fell back. But these leaders went even further. They decided that the bank would take a second look at every subprime loan application that a mortgage broker had submitted to Wells Fargo. Up to 60 percent of the overall mortgage financing at the time was being done through brokers.

If, based on the review of the credit information, it appeared that the borrower could qualify for a lower interest rate, the bank informed the borrower and recommended that she consult with her broker, who was copied on the written communication. A lot of brokers chose not to do business with Wells after that. As a result of these moves, the bank's market share declined from 2005 to 2007. The company estimates that it lost 2 to 4 percent in market share, or, for example, $50 billion to $100 billion in loan originations in 2006 alone. Heiden says:

I remember in our budget review the CEO saying, "How many businesses do we have where market share is declining?" And I'd have to raise my hand because our market share was declining, and we'd have to explain that, and sometimes we would get questions like, "Why aren't you good in this? You apparently aren't as good as the competition." And looking back, we were actually better in the long run, and it's being proven now. Now our market share is enjoying double-digit growth.

Our strategy is driving controlled, profitable, market share growth by building lasting relationships with customers and clients. Our vision is to help our customers achieve financial success. All the decisions we made in the subprime arena were totally aligned with this vision.

Wells Fargo chairman Dick Kovacevich was CEO as well during this time, and remembers clearly his tough line of questioning and his eventual decision to back up his team's decision. He knew the bank could have sold these kinds of bad loans and profited handsomely. But he chose not to become this kind of lender.

He backed Heiden's insistence that the company articulate its responsible lending principles for nonprime residential real estate lending so that everyone in the company knew them and lived them. Wells Fargo is a company where people feel empowered to make decisions, but these decisions are rooted in the company's vision and values "Bible" that goes out to every team member in every branch. Heiden's team added a section on "responsible lending" that said Wells Fargo would only approve an application when the company believed the borrower had the ability to repay the loan.

"And that protected us from this fiasco," Kovacevich told me. "We didn't do this, because in the long run we would have lost more money than we would have gained. Of course we shouldn't lend to someone who we know isn't going to be able to afford a loan, even if you can sell it to somebody else, because in the long run it's going to hurt us."

In the end, everyone won. The customers got better loans, the salespeople were reasonably compensated on loans that would not come back to haunt them, and the bank developed new relationships with appreciative new customers. Word of Wells Fargo's integrity spread throughout the industry.

Wells Fargo's love leadership showed that it was more concerned about a long-term win-win relationship with its customers than a short-term, potentially win-lose transaction with a one-time borrower.

Kovacevich emphasizes that the company's culture ultimately guides difficult decisions like these. By "culture" he means something more wide ranging that most companies: culture determines how the company's employees behave every day, and how they treat each other and their customers.

We believe so strongly in culture that we will not hire anybody, buy anybody, do a joint venture with anybody, unless we believe that the culture of that person or entity is compatible with us. For instance, when all the commercial banks in the 1990s were buying investment banks, we did not. It's not that investment banking wasn't a business. You could make money. It wasn't because our customers didn't want investment banking. It's that the cultures were incompatible. They were short-term oriented.

The reason we not only missed the subprime mortgage business, but we also missed the structured investment vehicles (SIVs) and the collateralized debt obligations (CDOs) and other things at the heart of the financial crisis is because we really were not in investment banking. It was culturally incompatible. And the fact that we treat people the way we do, that saved us from this culture of short-termism and greed. It's that simple.

Your culture tries to explain how you act every day without somebody telling you what to do. And we work so that people just know instinctively

how they should behave, how they should make
the right decisions when things are on the line.
If you establish that culture, employees know
exactly what to do, and therefore you can have
decentralized decision making and not be worried
that someone's crossing the line. And then who
gets promoted? The person who can teach that
culture, live that culture, communicate that culture
to people. That's who leads our company: not
someone who's the brightest or the smartest or
who makes the most money. Eventually, however,
they *will* make the most money.

Kovacevich's views come directly from his working-
class upbringing. He grew up in western Washington,
a land of dairy farmers, loggers, and sawmill workers.
Between the ages of eleven and eighteen, he worked in the
corner grocery store whenever he wasn't in school. It was
there that he learned that one of the most important things
is the last three feet between him and the customer. How
that customer was treated determined whether or not she
came back. As chairman and CEO of Norwest bank before
it merged with Wells Fargo, and then later at Wells Fargo
as chairman and CEO for almost ten years and since 2007
as chairman alone, he tried to make sure that everyone
who came into the bank was treated as a guest would be
treated in his own home.

Leaders operationalize these kinds of values through their people. Kovacevich told me that the bank creates a culture that prizes close relationships with customers, not through its executives alone, but also through its frontline workers:

I came from a lower-middle-class family. We never had enough money. We all knew we had to work to get what we had. But my parents would give their shirt and everything else off their back. No one worked harder.

And so I gained a respect for the common person. And as I got into the business world, I found that there was not a respect and appreciation for that group of people. And yet there were millions of them, and they were the base of the business. I asked, "What if you could get those people excited, motivated? They want to succeed, they want to work and give their creativity to the company."

People are a competitive advantage in our company. If you can get the people in your company to care more for their customers, their team members, their communities, and their stockholders than the people of our competitors, you win. Very simple.

Wells Fargo has outperformed the competition with a culture that infuses every level of the organization with love leadership.

■■

As Wells Fargo has learned, love fosters relationship-based business habits. In other words, it treats borrowers as valued long-term relationships rather than as indifferent and detached transactions. It's a mind-set that would have saved the rest of the banking industry billions of dollars in the mortgage meltdown and subsequent global financial crisis.

The basic cause of the crisis was a fundamental lack of a relationship with customers. The broker and the borrower in the mortgage deal were not really connected or committed in a real way; the broker and the banker were not really connected or committed; and this is key: the banker and the borrower were not connected or committed. Likewise, the banker and Wall Street were not connected or committed, and fatally, Wall Street securitization firms and the investors around the world to whom they sold these complex products were not connected or committed. There was no real relationship between any of these channels.

Put even more simply, as long as the broker, the banker, the Wall Street player, and others in the deal got their fee, they were happy—or so they thought. This behavior was further supercharged by shareholder pressure for firms to hit aggressive quarterly profit targets, a short-term focus that conveniently translated into huge performance bonuses for executives.

I am all for free enterprise and capitalism. Without a clearly defined profit motivation, a business simply will not be viable for long. My problem is that the relationship between all these various individuals and groups was simply the financial transaction. The concern was for the buck, not for the borrower.

In a healthy financial sector, the relationship should begin with the borrower, and connect in one direction to the broker, and connect in the other direction with all the individuals and groups that are tied together in the food chain. Instead, the focus became "I'm going to get mine, so you better get yours." The focus was not on the we, but on the me.

Everyone needs to have an enlightened self-interest in the outcome of a business transaction, and it should start with a genuine understanding of and concern with what's best for the client, the customer, the borrower. That concern—what I call love—was fundamentally absent during the events that led up to this economic crisis. There simply was no relationship with the borrower.

Wells Fargo, like most companies, is not perfect. But its key leadership constantly shows me that they are devoted to their mission to do right by their customers. At the time of this book's publication, there was a pending lawsuit against Wells Fargo tied to their subprime mortgage lending activities and allegations of discrimination. Whatever the outcome, what I know based on more than a decade working with Wells Fargo is that its leadership is committed to making wrongs right. And that's love leadership, too.

## U.S. Bank

Richard C. Hartnack, an Operation HOPE board member, understands well this problem of the transactional approach. He is in charge of consumer banking as vice chairman of US Bancorp, the Minneapolis-based parent company of US Bank, the sixth-largest commercial bank in America. Prior to that he served as vice chairman of Union Bank of California from 1991 to 2005.

US Bank was roundly criticized in 2006 and 2007 for having slower revenue growth than many of its peer banks. A big reason was its decision to largely ignore the mortgage market, except for the prime loans that it had mostly specialized in.

Hartnack recalls that when the financial crisis hit in 2007, US Bank took a hard look at its adjustable rate mortgage (ARM) loans. The bank didn't make these loans with the intention that they were going to be a problem, but it saw in September 2007 that interest rates at that time were expected to go up. The bank did the math and knew that the change in the rates would be a big a shock to its mortgage holders.

U.S. Bank had a choice: it could try to deal individually with thousands of households and figure out the exact right loan for each one, and while it was doing that, could watch people get into serious trouble paying their loans. Or the bank could simply not raise the rates.

Hartnack knew that the bank was either going to have to deal with a lot of bad loans, or it could make this concession and see a set of problems just go away. The bank opted for love leadership. It held the interest rate steady, and told customers they had to opt out of their ARM into a fixed interest rate. And as you would expect, a large percentage of the bank's clients accepted the offer.

Hartnack's decision turned out to be prescient, one that did well for the bank and did good for its customers. It helped people stay in affordable mortgages, and it avoided foreclosures, where everyone loses. He says:

> This example is proof that a short-term focus has a lot of temptations. It's a rare set of circumstances—combining the board of directors, CEO, top management, investors, analysts, the culture, and everything else—that creates an environment in which people are willing to look at the long haul and avoid short-term temptations. When you're operating for the short term, there are a thousand little trade-offs where you find yourself faced with choices that are terribly uncomfortable. And it

takes a huge amount of character on the part of a management team to stand up to those.

In the end, all you really have is your reputation. When you're dead and buried, they're not going to bury your money with you. When you're dead and gone, what people are going to look back on is your reputation, and people are going to judge if you're a leader in business with your customers, your community, your employees, and your shareholders.

Your reputation depends on something greater than making money. It depends on creating prosperity for all.

## DOING GOOD

Building long-term relationships based on genuine care is not enough. The third law of love leadership, love makes money, involves your *purpose* in business. As I learned from my days of hustling as an entrepreneur, that purpose must be to do good if you want sustainable prosperity and yes, money, to be a measurable by-product of your business.

I recently attended a dinner in Vienna, Austria, and a businessman leaned over to me and said, "The greatest sin is not to do bad. All men will do bad, thus all men will sin. The greatest sin is not to do good, when you could."

I don't believe that you can love unless you do the hard work of circulating that love. Love follows one of the primary laws of money: currency without circulation has no value. Likewise, love without circulation has no value. Love is an action. Love is doing. The action necessary is doing good.

Crown Prince Haakon is the heir apparent to the throne of Norway, cofounder with me and Professor Pekka Himanen of the organization Global Dignity, and a fellow YGL. Prince Haakon explains:

> It's deeply human to want to do good. If we're separated from that deep need to do good for other people, something essential is lost. And I would say the same thing for companies. If a company separates doing good for people and making a profit, and then cuts out the doing good part, something essential is lost. Gandhi said that if you look at all leaders doing bad things, with time, they all fall. Only good things persist over time.
>
> The most precious asset any person has is not their money, not their job, not even their family. I think the most precious asset people have is their own life. And it's the question we all need to ask ourselves: What do I want to use this precious asset for?
>
> If you really are serious about contributing something good in this world, then that will influence the way you live your family life, it will influence the

way you do your job, it will influence the choices you make in your professional career. It influences everything if you're really serious about using your life, your most precious asset, to do good.

Crown Prince Haakon reminds us that good things persist and that our purpose then must be to do good. The money will follow from this orientation over the long term.

My friend the late Jack Kemp, former nine-term Republican congressman, one-time vice-presidential candidate, and former secretary of housing and urban development, made this connection even more concrete:

As a young boy growing up in Los Angeles, I was always taught that the opposite of love is not hate. It's indifference. Indifference to people in poverty, or to your neighbor who's down and out, was the real sin. But it also leaves you with a business plan that is ultimately unsuccessful.

When people see your compassion, your concern, your caring for those less fortunate, they will see in your example a force for good in society. And you will be rewarded—in contracts, in business, in everything.

Leaders like Kemp know that love leadership creates its own rewards. You do good, you look at the long term, you build real relationships based on genuine caring for others. These make you happy *and* successful.

Sure, the return on this investment of time and effort is money, but it's also a whole lot more. Money is the by-product of love leadership. True wealth is its ultimate reward.

The desire to attain true wealth is a universal theme throughout the history of mankind, and is a far more deeply embedded human need than that of simply accumulating money. If you can put your love into circulation, you can achieve not just the accumulation of money but also true wealth, which I define as spiritual wealth, intellectual wealth, and emotional wealth—*plus* some money, which tends to naturally follow the other qualities of true wealth.

Following the third law of love leadership will make you wealthy and wise. But to truly gain wisdom—and the power that comes from that—you need to understand yourself, as we'll see in the next law of love leadership.

# 4

# VULNERABILITY
# IS POWER

By mid-2008, Operation HOPE was beginning to feel the effects of the growing financial crisis gripping our nation and soon to spread around the globe. HOPE partners in the financial sector were under severe pressure; some were merging with other companies and in some cases even shutting down overnight. This was a scary time for a nonprofit organization like ours that is nearly 100 percent partner financed.

Although no partner canceled its commitment to HOPE, almost every one began to slow payments to the organization. One of our substantial funders told me that it had approved our grant, but needed to sit on the funding until the last minute. It was stockpiling cash for itself during this period. This was breathtaking news to hear, as we needed the cash more than this large company did.

At the end of 2008, almost $2 million in near-term 2008 revenue we had budgeted for was either missing, delayed, rescheduled for 2009, or never to be granted as hoped. That amount was more than 15 percent of our cash budget, and represented money needed for operations; it was not simply a paper loss. Even some members of my board of directors were gently suggesting that HOPE was going to face a rough road ahead. Support for charitable organizations like ours would decline significantly, they predicted. A sharp scaling back of plans, and even more drastic options, were under serious consideration.

I did not share this view. In fact, I saw the potential for the largest surge in growth for Operation HOPE in our seventeen-year history. In the midst of the worst economic crisis in at least a generation, HOPE and our agenda were more relevant today than ever before.

In the short term, I was managing our balance sheet, reducing debt, and increasing reserves. One day while going over our budget, I discovered that we were missing revenue from two sources that we thought had been secure. Two things had happened. The CEO of a Fortune 500 company had committed $350,000 to me, but, unfortunately, he had gotten fired. The pledge had not yet been documented, so it would have been hard to make the case to the company that this was a commitment it had to accept. To do so would be winning battles and losing wars, so I decided to let the $350,000 go.

There is a longer story behind the second sum, $650,000, which was a renewal from a major credit card company that some advocates I respected had viewed as a predatory lender. When I first started dealing with this company, its executives struck me as left-brain turnaround artists, numbers-only guys who understood Wall Street but not the day-to-day concerns of people on Main Street. What they did wasn't technically illegal, but it was unethical. They were taking advantage of poor people who are financially illiterate.

I said to the CEO, "I'm going to assume that you are not a bad guy. I'm going to assume that you've done some bad things, but that you're a good person and you want to make it right. Let me help you run a better company."

I didn't judge him, because from a practical standpoint, I knew that if I hung around only upstanding individuals, I wouldn't be able to help the poor people who are in the portfolios of companies like his. Remember, the people Jesus hung around with weren't always saints. "A saint is a sinner that got up," says my friend Bishop Kenneth Ulmer, senior pastor-teacher of Faithful Central Bible Church in Inglewood, California. In order for me to get to the financially unprepared people this company was targeting, I needed to find a way to appeal to this executive's fundamental goodness and his sense of enlightened self-interest.

I gave the company the benefit of the doubt and proposed to work with it on a consulting basis only. A partnership with HOPE would have to wait. We would make recommendations for improving the firm's business practices so as to help it act more ethically. The hitch was that the company's executives wanted to issue press releases in our name and to have our logo on its Web site. We wanted to slow down and make sure we were on the same page before entering into any form of partnership.

I believe in what I now call the Oprah Rule. I remember when Oprah Winfrey was considering inviting me on her show and making me one of her "Oprah's Angel Network" awardees. Her office sent a private investigator out to chat with me. That guy checked me out more thoroughly than the Secret Service at the White House ever did. That was smart of Oprah, and I respected her for doing that. To me, Oprah was saying that she didn't want to publicly put her arms around anyone who did not have as much to lose as she did.

I passed the test. Oprah made me one of her Oprah's Angels, and she donated $100,000 to Operation HOPE, which I subsequently used to open our Chicago office in her honor. I also adopted the Oprah Rule at HOPE, believing that we had to do business with credible, honorable companies that had as much to lose in terms of their reputation as we did. If something went wrong with a client in the underserved communities where we worked, we wanted to be sure they would bend over backward to make it right.

But unbeknownst to me, people at the credit card company we were considering advising had talked some of our executives at HOPE into drafting a memorandum of understanding (MOU) for a full partnership. They had a press release ready to go, and had floated the idea with my team that a check for an additional several hundred thousand dollars would come with the signing of the MOU. My people put it all in front of me to sign.

"We can't do this," I said. "We hope they're going to take our recommendations, but they haven't done that yet. We can't just take them on their word. We've got to take them on their actions. Remember, our clients are poor people, not rich companies."

Unlike in the episode recounted in Chapter Two, when I stood up on my desk and shouted at my staff, this time I responded differently. I gently pushed the MOU away from me and said, "I'm not signing this. Either they write the check to us for our consulting services, period, with no acknowledgment by HOPE of them publicly, or we walk away from the deal." The company's executives were not happy, but to their credit, they wrote that first six-figure check.

We gave the company our recommendations, but then later that year, the FDIC sued it for $54 million for deceptive business practices. That company is now in a death spiral and will most likely be purchased or liquidated. We decided not to accept a renewal of the relationship that would have led to a partnership. We turned down the money, which created that $650,000 hole in our 2008 revenue budget.

Meanwhile, we lived to fight another day. We didn't lose our integrity, our reputation, or our soul. They are priceless. If we had partnered with this firm publicly, the dent in our character would have kept us from being able to raise money from credible sources, or do business credibly in the communities we serve.

At this point, our reserves were declining faster than I would have liked. We needed to call an emergency session of the board to deal with the shortfall.

## VULNERABILITY AND TRANSPARENCY

How I communicate with my board of directors is a lesson in the fourth law of love leadership, vulnerability is power. I tend to overcommunicate, even at the risk of irritating some people. I would rather tell my board members what they don't need to hear than risk not telling them something they thought I should have. I would rather overcommunicate, undercommit, and overperform than undercommunicate, overcommit, and underperform. Board members have to trust the people who are operating the organization to give them both good news *and* bad news in real time. They need transparency.

Leaders demonstrate their character and build integrity, credibility, and trust by how they work through problems and manage pain. When I have bad news, the board knows I'll tell them, and I'll tell them quickly. I take responsibility and then set out to *change* things.

This approach is based on vulnerability and transparency, and is precisely the opposite of what fear tells a leader to do when faced with bad news. In dire situations, many so-called leaders become like deer caught in the headlights, unable or unwilling to be honest about the situation and to make critical decisions quickly and with a level of clarity, accountability, and openness, let alone with a forward-looking vision.

The love-leadership approach to managing problems and bad news is different, and it pays dividends. It brings people along with you and helps them buy in. It operates from vulnerability and transparency rather than pride and secrecy. Often this vulnerability gives others the comfort and confidence to stay with you when things get really rough.

The fourth law of love leadership—vulnerability is power—says that admitting weaknesses and owning up to mistakes have counterintuitive benefits. When you are honest, people are more likely to forgive you any weaknesses and mistakes. You are also able to make a stronger connection with others. That ultimately gives you an ability to persuade and influence people, which in turn strengthens your ability to lead.

Things got pretty rough at HOPE in late 2008. It was one of the toughest operating environments I have seen in seventeen years of running the organization. I drafted a two-page memorandum to Operation HOPE's board warning them of my concerns and rallying them to help me "manage my balance sheet" during these challenging times. And then I got on the phone with our executive board of directors.

I told them the bad news first: short-term debt had increased, and reserves had decreased beyond where I was comfortable. In addition to slow accounts receivable, the problem was the $1 million shortfall in promised revenue, and I told them exactly why it had happened. I said that there are over six billion people on the planet, and we would simply need to talk to someone else. There would be other opportunities and other checks. But we wouldn't get a second chance at character, at ethics, at our reputation.

Then I told them my plan for turning things around. I said that people were right about charitable giving going down, but they were wrong that it had to go down for HOPE. I believed there would be a mass pullback, and once we survived that, there would be a reassessment and a cautious move back into the market with a clear "flight to quality."

Operation HOPE has always sought to be to community economic empowerment what Tiger Woods is to golf, what Michael Jordan was and remains to basketball, what Bill and Melinda Gates are now to philanthropy—a "best in class" player. We are also betting on the long term. Immediately after everyone's economic houses stopped burning, the next question out of the mouths of consumers and leaders would be, "How do we make sure that a mess like this never happens again?"

The work of Operation HOPE would be a big part of that answer. In short, I predicted we would be busier and more relevant than ever before. My plan was to raise

$25 million in long-term capital for our work here in the United States, and another $5 million for our work in South Africa. This represents the largest investment campaign for HOPE in our entire history, and it is being launched during a time when others are saying the sky is falling and that I should be ducking, not sticking my neck out.

Most people around me simply saw an economy in free fall and bad news all around them, but I saw something entirely different. They were looking at the results of the actions of the past, through the rearview mirror, but I was looking at a practical vision for the future, through the front window. At the heart of this economic crisis was a massive level of borrower and consumer financial illiteracy and all-around greed. The predators who sold us all those bad and overly sophisticated loan products had a little inside help—from us.

I was not paralyzed with fear. After nearly two decades in the vineyards of HOPE, my vision of financial literacy as a new civil right—and the first in a series of global silver rights—would finally have relevance, for everyone.

After I had outlined all this to the board, I braced myself for an avalanche of criticism. But to a member, each agreed with the board member who said, "John, you played this exactly right. Your plan makes a lot of sense. And bravo to you for walking away from that $650,000."

All I could think was "Wow." I knew I was doing the right thing, but in all honesty I did not know that the board would back me. And that is what I mean when I say that courage is nothing more than your faith reaching through your fear.

Two weeks after that call, every board member responded positively, and generously offered to help us resolve the challenges we faced, even though they were dealing with challenges within their own organizations at the same time. People rally around individuals who show transparency and display the character to lead, partly because it reinforces the character they want to see infused within their own operating environments.

I remember going to lunch recently with one of my new board members, Robert Burton, president of E\*TRADE Bank and chief operating officer of E\*TRADE. I asked him why the company had kept its ten-year, $10 million commitment to HOPE, even while the company was being buffeted in the financial markets.

His answer was simple: "We made a commitment to the community, and we must keep it." I will remember those words for the rest of my career. The response says more about E\*TRADE and its people than any fancy commercial or press release about its superior products. With those few words, I was a customer for life.

In the end, not only did we hit our mark of securing $2 million to balance our budget for 2008, but as of early 2009, we have secured a $7 million cash commitment from a new and credible partner in financial services along with a $5 million in-kind commitment for national media outreach from a leading communications company—in the midst of the most severe world economic crisis since the Great Depression. The new funds are equivalent to more than 90 percent of our organizational budget for all of 2008.

Remember that $25 million in long-term funding support I said I would secure for HOPE in 2009? We are well on our way to achieving that goal, with a little faith, a lot of hard work, and a commitment to love leadership through good times and bad.

We never gave up on our dreams, our values, or our belief in ourselves. We were awake to opportunity, even in the midst of a terrible storm. And we were vulnerable. Combine these qualities with a rock-solid plan, a proven product, and an inspiring vision for our collective future, and there's nothing we can't achieve.

Remember: "Fear is a prosperity killer."

## WHY VULNERABILITY IS A SOURCE OF POWER

Some people might say that opening up with my board in such a vulnerable way might have made me look weak. Real leaders, however, understand that vulnerability can actually become their greatest strength.

When you open up, people open up to you. Vulnerability is the door to your heart, and being vulnerable grants important benefits to those who are strong enough to leave that door open. Vulnerability shows that you are human, and it makes you loved—and all great leaders are, at their core, deeply human and much loved. That's why people follow them. *It's the source of their power.*

119

As my mentor the Reverend Murray confirms:

Vulnerability is power. You can face the mountain
with fear and trembling, even as those who
follow your leadership. But what great respect,
admiration, and love they have for you when you
take the post position nonetheless and beckon
them to follow, "Mountain, get out of my way!"

If you're vulnerable, people follow your lead. As
H. H. Brookins, bishop of the African Methodist Episcopal
Church, once told me, "If you think you're a leader and
you turn around and there's nobody behind you, you're
not a leader, you're just a guy out taking a walk."

When it comes to attracting followers, the power of
influence always trumps the power of coercion. You pull
people in your direction, rather than push them. They follow you because they are drawn to your authenticity and
your actions.

Rather than ceding control to others, being vulnerable
actually puts you in the driver's seat. You're not waiting
around for anyone else to open up, to get in touch, to care.
You see what's needed and you do it, out of care for others.
When you love, you're taking charge of the situation, even
if it makes you vulnerable. In fact, you're almost always
vulnerable when you love, because love pries you open and
makes people in need seek you out.

Coercion gains you only compliance, but influence
is about gaining real, sustainable power in the world and

above-the-line performance from people. Before you know it, people in your organization are working overtime and weekends, and bugging you with e-mails at midnight with their newest, greatest idea. But you get to the table of influence only through the door of vulnerability and love leadership. In other words, people will meet you where you are. If you give 50 percent, they will do just about the same in return.

David L. Brewer III knows the feeling of being vulnerable. Brewer is the former superintendent of the Los Angeles Unified School District, which is the second-largest school district in America with more than 712,000 students; eight hundred schools; seventy-seven thousand employees; and a $7.5 billion budget. Before that he was a three-star vice admiral who served in the U.S. Navy for thirty-five years. He now cochairs the Los Angeles chapter of Five Million Kids, Operation HOPE's initiative to break the high school dropout epidemic in America.

One of the most compelling moments of Brewer's life was hearing a speech that Rev. Dr. Martin Luther King gave when Brewer was at Howard University. In that speech, Dr. King made a compelling point. He said, "I love everybody, but I don't like everybody." Dr. King was speaking about love as respect.

Brewer had a chance to learn that lesson when he served in the U.S. Navy. When he first joined the Navy in 1970, there were only 250 African American officers out of a total of 72,000. Needless to say, he needed to have a lot of love-leadership relationships in order to ascend the ranks in the Navy:

> I'll never forget one of my toughest, most defining tours, as chief engineer on the USS *Okinawa*, which was an amphibious assault helicopter ship. When I walked aboard that ship as an African American, all the senior noncommissioned officers I would lead were white. (We call them chief petty officers in the United States Navy.) They would go down into their living quarters, "goat locker," as we called it, which is an area on the ship where they would eat, sleep and speak frankly with each other. And word came back to me from the goat locker that some of my chief petty officers had said, "We will not work for 'that nigger.'"
>
> And so I had two choices. I could either love them or like them. If I had chosen to like them, I would have fired them. But I chose to love them and to basically respect them as human beings and get beyond their own prejudices. In other words, I took their prejudice and turned it into power.
>
> I basically got those racist chief petty officers to work for me, because I showed them my own competence. But more important, I basically respected them as human beings and professionals

and showed them how to do their jobs better and to be successful human beings. And as a result of my love, four of the guys who were in dead-end careers were promoted. Now, they never liked me and some of them will probably never like me, but they all loved me for that.

Brewer has learned something vitally important about climbing up the ranks: "True leaders are ladder builders; they're not ladder climbers," he told me recently. "The ladder builder is always saying, 'What can I do to help you? How would I make you successful?' If you make your team successful, your team's going to make you successful."

The way to climb that ladder is through vulnerability, Brewer says:

> Good leaders are vulnerable. The bottom line is, you admit your vulnerability—that you're going to make mistakes, and you're going to screw up— and then that opens people up to you. But more important, people will now feel free to express themselves to you and take you to the next level. They will tell you when you are nakedly wrong and you have no clothes on. And you need that, because ultimately, success is not about you in the first place. Success is about others, and it's about the mission and the organization.

I once knew a ladder climber in the Navy who was all about himself. This master chief petty officer would con sailors and treat them badly. And sure enough, he made it all the way to the top of the ranks. When he was charged with sexual harassment and he called all of us pleading to be character witnesses for him, nobody stepped forward: none of the sailors who worked for him, none of the officers for whom he had worked. He ended up getting a bad conduct discharge, was busted in rank, and lost all of his retirement after almost thirty years of service.

When you make mistakes, you're going to fall. And when ladder climbers make mistakes, there are no steps below to catch them when they fall. They broke all of those steps walking on the backs of all those people on the way up to the top. And now there's no one to catch them.

If you are a true ladder builder, you have built strong steps. You have built strong people as you have ascended that ladder.

As Brewer explains, admitting your mistakes is a critical way to show vulnerability. You admit that you aren't perfect and don't have all the answers. When you are vulnerable in this way, people are more likely to forgive you any missteps and come to your aid—you are more likely to make a deeper connection. This is precisely why being vulnerable is being powerful.

## HOW TO SHOW VULNERABILITY

Delivering bad news and admitting mistakes as soon as you become aware of them is one of the most powerful ways to show vulnerability. At a practical level, the fourth law of love leadership—vulnerability is power—translates into how I deal with bad news, which is *directly*. Bad news does not go away just because I don't want to deal with it. Generally, I find that bad news only gets worse if it's left to drift on its own.

Love is work, and doing the work means dealing with bad news before it deals with you.

Why wait for someone to whom you owe money to call you? You knew Tuesday you didn't have it. Surprise him and give him a ring first, saying, "Joe, I don't have the $100 I owe you, and I won't have it until next month, but I do have $20 today, and I want to send it to you today." Calling him first is the entire ball game, because if he has to track you down, he has also already assumed you are a bum with no intention of making good on your commitments.

This philosophy works whether you are a single mother dealing with a $100 telephone bill, a CEO running a multinational corporation with unexpected bad news for your board, a Wall Street investor who traded on what is now known to be inside information, or the leader of the free world.

I remember in 2001 when entertainment diva Martha Stewart was charged with insider trading. She sold her holding of ImClone stock to avoid a loss the day before the company reported that an important drug had failed to receive FDA approval. The entire sad affair could have been avoided if she had simply said, "I am embarrassed. I admit that in a moment of panic, I took information I now know to be insider information, and I sold stocks that I should not have because I expected a loss on them if I didn't. I screwed up, and I am sorry. I hope the public will forgive me this transgression."

What would have happened? Probably a fine from the SEC and at most a misdemeanor slap on the wrist, and she would have been back on her hit cooking show without missing a beat. But that is not what happened. Stewart did not want to do the work. She did not want to admit she screwed up. She did not make herself vulnerable. She ducked instead.

She danced around with words and generally peeved government prosecutors, whose annual salaries at their jobs were a fraction of what she made in a week. She destroyed her goodwill and created an environment in which individuals who protect the public good felt a need to throw the book at her, to teach her and others like her a lesson, and to send a message to the public. They did and she paid dearly, with five months in jail, five months of home confinement, and a $30,000 fine.

There was a better way. In this situation, the fourth law of love leadership simply made good common sense, and would have saved Stewart money, jail time, and a damaged reputation. Of course, she is doing just fine now, because she is brilliant and genuinely talented at what she does, but her career today represents a mere fraction of the success she once enjoyed.

Contrast Stewart with Michael Critelli, who is the former executive chairman and CEO of Pitney Bowes and is now active in the public and private sector around the issues of health and health care, transportation and sustainable infrastructure development, and community development. He says:

> Honesty is most tested when you have to admit mistakes and humble yourself. But it's also the time when you get the most credibility and mileage because people empathize with you. They know that it's painful, and they will cut you a break.

> You've got to somehow figure out a way to say, "I'm a vulnerable human being. I made a mistake. I am not infallible." And most people are going to be forgiving in those circumstances. I've been very candid when I've made mistakes at Pitney Bowes. Once you say that, it's very hard for someone to stay angry at you.

127

Critelli says that being as up-front and honest as possible is just plain good business strategy. As a communications consultant once told him, telling the truth was most important because, whereas a stock price could recover from a hit, Critelli's credibility, if lost, could not recover. He remembers a call in October 2000 when he had to tell investors about the ultimate bad news: a shortfall in earnings. There were a lot of angry people on the call, because the stock had dropped by 35 percent in one day.

On that call, he told investors that although the company looks at a lot of data and analysis about the business, which have historically not let the company down, something new was happening that was inconsistent with anything that had happened previously. He promised to do better, and—equally important in these situations—he said that earnings could fall short again. The company would reduce the risk of a mistake, but it could never eliminate it.

Over the years, he has found that investors who otherwise would have left stayed with Pitney Bowes because the company was extremely honest about the past, present, and future. He says you have to be honest and credible on all three fronts if you want to stay in business. That's what vulnerability is all about.

## MAKING DEEP CONNECTIONS THROUGH VULNERABILITY

Critelli knows that when you are vulnerable, you are able to build a stronger connection with others, and therefore you are able to persuade and influence them. They will stick with you because of this bond.

We see this every day in our work at Operation HOPE. As part of our mission, we frequently talk with students in inner-city schools about financial literacy and those kids' real inner wealth—dignity. With each conversation, we strive to create a connection between successful leaders and students from poor neighborhoods. The way we create that connection between two seemingly disconnected groups is by opening up and being vulnerable. Anything else creates more friction and distance.

If I were to walk into a classroom and start talking about my credentials and how many powerful people I knew, it would instantly turn off an audience of inner-city kids. They already feel bad enough about their situation, so who am I to make them feel worse about what they're not doing and how supposedly great I am?

Their arms would start to fold in front of them. And when people's arms fold, it is a signal that they're turning off, retreating, becoming defensive. That's not helpful. You want their arms to drop, preferably with one hand on each leg in a relaxed, attentive posture. You want them to smile and laugh, because laughter is the way into the heart and the soul. You want them to be vulnerable and open, and that process starts with you. Remember, a school's curriculum has never taught a child anything. An inspiring and passionate teacher who makes a connection, aided by an informed curriculum, teaches and transforms that child.

So I mix seriousness with jokes. And I open up. I talk about race, my failures in my life, the divorce of my mom and dad, and being homeless. I talk about how even in my own life, loss has created what some people see as a leader. But I am sure also to talk about them—their aspirations and their dreams, their true worth. No one really wants to hear about you; people want to hear about themselves.

I also pay attention to the teachers, telling them that they are both underpaid and underappreciated, but that they are nurturing future young heroes and sheroes who could each change the world. The kids and teachers alike often erupt in applause *for themselves*. Particularly in tough times like these, people need someone to reaffirm that they matter.

At the end of some talks, I get standing ovations and hugs afterward. Even though I didn't know the audience before, we all feel like friends after an hour of a love-leadership conversation.

I once had the opportunity to take Alan Greenspan, at that time chairman of the Federal Reserve, to talk to students in an Operation HOPE financial literacy class in a middle school in inner-city Washington, D.C. His staff briefed me about the meeting beforehand, telling me what I could not do: I could not hug him, I could not talk about religion, I could not talk about this and that. The list was endless—and pointless.

Anyone who knows me knows that I'm naturally a hugger, and I like to talk openly about spirituality, so I said, "Gee, what can I talk about with this guy? You've got my hands tied."

And they said, "The markets listen to what the chairman says, and the chairman's going to have prepared remarks." These kids could have cared less about that, and would have gone to sleep at their desks. I had to help save this man from himself and his overly concerned aides.

Before the classroom visit, Greenspan and I had a semi-private meeting, and when I first saw him, I just hugged him. And I said that in my opinion, "There's a difference between being broke and being poor. Being broke is a temporary situation; being poor is a disabling frame of mind. We must vow never to be poor again." At its heart, it was a comment about lifting people's spirits, and the staff got all bent out of shape that this smacked of spirituality.

And then right before we went in to talk with the kids, the chairman got a little vulnerable himself and said, "John, what do you recommend I talk about with these kids?"

I was vulnerable, too, and I first admitted that I didn't have all the answers. I said, "I don't know what you should say. None of us knows. But if I were you, the first thing I'd do is put down that prepared speech. If you want to put these kids to sleep, give them a speech about financial literacy."

I explained that people don't want a mortgage; they want to become a home owner. People don't want a car loan; they want a cool car. And people don't want an education; they want what an education can give them. I told Greenspan to simply tell his story, to talk about how he grew up.

"These kids think you're a rich, old, powerful white man who they can't relate to, and that they're poor, black, and hopeless, because a lot of them have self-esteem issues and have not been affirmed in their lives," I said. "Often people have talked to them about success and strength. How about we flip the script and talk about success as vulnerability and show these kids you can make a mistake and not *be* a mistake? That even when you fall, you fall forward, and that success is going from failure to failure without a loss of enthusiasm."

And he looked at me and said, "OK, let's do that."

We went into the classroom, and I did one more thing his staff hated. I got the kids interested in his story, my way. I told them he had learned statistics through baseball cards; that his mother had given him an allowance, which was how he got interested in business; and that he studied music at Juilliard and at one time was passionate about becoming a jazz artist. Greenspan didn't have what it takes to be a professional performer, I said, so instead he began to prepare tax returns for members of the band. And today, from that humble beginning, he was chairman of the

Federal Reserve, able to move markets with his every word and one of the most powerful men in the world. Go figure.

Then I said, "I've been hanging around the chairman, and you know, I think he's a pretty cool guy. I think we should make him an honorary black man!" And the mostly African American kids in the audience just laughed their heads off. Laughter is a tonic and a connector of spirits. Laughter also lowers false barriers and allows us to relate to each other. The kids relaxed, the chairman relaxed, and all the tension just went right out of the room. That was enough to create a bridge between Greenspan and these kids, and then the magic began. They started talking about their common experiences.

Initially, the chairman was so uncomfortable in this highly unstructured, inner-city environment that instead of talking out of the small wireless mic that was on his lapel, he had the transmitter in his hand turned upside down, and was talking into the bottom of it. I had to gently pull the unit out of his hand, turn it around, and ask him to put it in his pocket. He could not have been more gracious with me.

After that he relaxed and started talking about his life, from his childhood experiences forward, and how that related to what he was doing now. He talked about how if he could do it, they could do it. In an hour, they were like old friends. The kids learned about the language of money, gained some self-confidence, were inspired, and felt better about themselves. And they had a relationship with the chairman of the Federal Reserve.

They were all better because of the experience. They also figured out that they weren't so different. They all wanted the same thing: they wanted to succeed. The chairman was valued and valuable, and so were they.

When you get real with people, when you show vulnerability, you connect with them and you move them on a human level. That gives you real power.

## THE COURAGE TO BE VULNERABLE

People meet you where you are. If you're open, they tend to be open. If you're closed, they tend to be closed. If you're vulnerable, they tend to be vulnerable. And people are often a little insecure and afraid of themselves. They're afraid to tip their hand. It's just human nature, self-preservation. People will generally only tip their hand when they see you tip your hand.

Of course, you can play it safe, but you will never get to the real richness of that relationship until you tip your hand. The real friends you meet were friends from the very first time, and the acquaintances you meet remain acquaintances for a lifetime. That acquaintance is only an acquaintance because you two have just been cordial with each other, talking about the weather for years. You are never really comfortable with that person. But with that best friend you met, you developed a deep connection almost instantly. It didn't take any work—it was just instantaneous, it was magic. And you found yourself in a long conversation about real-life things. You were coming from the same place. You were both being vulnerable and open.

That is the essence of leadership. Love leadership is about marshaling courage. And the confidence to have courage is a sign of faith in spite of your fear. That's what makes leaders unique—leaders will put aside fear and do what most people are not inclined to do. When everyone is going left, leaders go right. They take the road less traveled.

Most people close down in tough times, whereas leaders open up in tough times. Most people see a risk and want to close a hand and create a fist. A leader will open her hand and create openness in a dialogue. Someone who leads based on fear sees war as the only way to achieve his ends. But a true leader sees prosperity as the pathway to peace, and war as the failure to negotiate.

Vulnerability creates that mutual prosperity. It gives you real power.

The path to love leadership is not through a closed fist of battle. It's through an open hand of giving. And there's a benefit to this openness. As we'll see in the next chapter, when you give, you get.

# 5

# GIVING
# IS GETTING

Operation HOPE is a love story," says my friend Bill Walbrecher, president and chief operating officer of Operation HOPE. He was talking about my strategic operating plan for Operation HOPE in late 2008, but he just as easily could have been describing the philosophy of our entire organization. Walbrecher is a hard-nosed former CEO of a Fortune 500 bank, so when he uses a word like *love* in a sentence, you've got to believe that something important is going on.

As I described in the previous chapter, by late 2008 Operation HOPE was facing a major revenue crunch as a direct result of the global economic crisis. HOPE partners were under severe financial pressure, and many times we felt it almost instantly, as partners began to slow or cancel payments to the organization. In addition to leaving a $2 million hole in our $15 million annual budget, we faced a pressing need for me to return almost full-time to the organization in September 2008 to raise additional capital for our work and to manage our balance sheet.

I had been away from HOPE for a good part of 2008, focusing on making the promises of the recently enacted U.S. President's Advisory Council on Financial Literacy—of which I am vice chairman, working alongside my friend Charles Schwab, who serves as chairman—relevant to the lives of ordinary Americans. The council was the direct result of the leadership work of Operation HOPE, but it was obvious that HOPE needed me to return once again. The organization had to tighten its financial belt. I needed to push and inspire our team to do more with less, and that started with me setting the example: I worked longer hours than ever before.

When I said earlier that our budget shortfall was leading us to consider a sharp scaling back of plans, I wasn't telling the full story. What I could have done, and what some might say I should have done, was lay off employees and close service offices. I chose not to, and during late 2008, we never laid off a single employee or closed an office.

The result of all these decisions translated into more stress on me and my senior management team. I was the one charged with raising 100 percent of the additional funding we needed to survive. My senior management team was dealing with greater levels of organizational stress, because they had to grapple with the real effects of tightening financial resources on the ground and with their people.

Let me say it plain: it would have been much easier to have simply cited the recession's impact on our finances, and thereafter rapidly moved to cut a significant percentage of our staff, services, and program offices. I know many leaders who would not have thought twice about axing employees to boost the bottom line. But that did not make sense to me, or make it right. This approach more often than not ends up winning battles and losing wars.

To me, people in our staff are not numbers on a page. They are friends and dedicated employees. They are mothers and fathers, proud providers for their families, and human beings. Our paycheck pays the mortgage, the car note, the insurance, and the grocery bill. Although they are fairly compensated to be sure, most of them still live from paycheck to paycheck, just as approximately 70 percent of all Americans do. They love helping others, and most would do the work for free if they could afford to, but as a practical matter they also need this job to provide dignity, shelter, education, and hope for themselves and their families.

The people in the underserved communities we serve also desperately need the programs and services of HOPE now more than ever. Just one look at the fifty-seven thousand calls we have received to our Mortgage HOPE Crisis Hotline alone, and the $200 million in mortgages we have helped to restructure or modify for individuals struggling against foreclosure, was all the proof I needed to understand the profound impact of our work. And so, if I could at all avoid it, I did not want to reduce services at the very time when individuals, increasingly including middle-class individuals, needed the hope and opportunity for dignity we offered.

Even when surrounded by bad economic news, our workers were surprisingly confident about the future and filled with personal satisfaction about their noble calling, the meaningful work they were doing, and the contribution to society they were making. They felt secure knowing that this was more than a job. For my part, I felt good about the sacrifices we were making for our people, and if I had to work a little harder and carry a bit more stress, it was a small price to pay.

My sense of commitment to our team back then has already paid dividends, as I have never seen them more committed, more passionate, harder working, or more effective today. They were right there with me when I needed them most, and I am so deeply honored. We have exceeded our fundraising targets, have so far closed no offices, and have laid off no employees. Ninety-nine percent of our partners renewed their commitment to our work in 2008.

This is love leadership in action. This is truly an example of the power of an organization that has spent seventeen years building relationships, character, credibility, and an authentic voice, serving and empowering others, including our partners. This is the long-term power of love leadership to pay dividends years after the fact.

## THE MORE YOU GIVE, THE MORE YOU GET

The message of this story is the premise behind the fifth law of love leadership: giving is getting. The more you give, the more you get. Rather than firing employees, I worked even harder. As a leader, I gave more and got much more in return. As a leader, I also gave to the citizens we served. Both types of giving are key elements of servant leadership.

As a servant leader, you are a steward of the resources—human, financial, and otherwise—that your organization provides. Leaders serve those inside and outside the organization and at the same time focus on achieving results in line with the organization's mission and values. Robert Greenleaf first coined the concept of servant leadership in 1977 in terms of employees, but the concept has been expanded much more widely. He wrote, "The best test, and difficult to administer, is: do those served grow as persons? Do they grow while being served, become healthier, wiser, freer, more autonomous, more likely themselves to become servants?"[1]

Former president Bill Clinton explained the concept of servant leadership to me this way:

> In order to be a true leader, you need to have a deep passion for helping the people you're leading. If you don't really see yourself as a servant leader, you won't make decisions that benefit those who

141

put you there. The servant leader's scorecard is simple—Are people better off when you quit than when you started? Were the poor and powerless a part of the progress, and is there a stronger sense that our common humanity is more important than our interesting differences?

Politics is very much a "getting" business. You have to get support, contributions, and votes, over and over again. But most important, I have been given wonderful, improbable opportunities by the American people, which have, in turn, allowed me the opportunity to give back. I think that in order to be successful and live a full, rewarding life, you must do what you can to balance the scales by using what's given to you to give back to others.

The fifth law of love leadership translates into a long-term commitment to serving others, starting with serving those who work in your organization and expanding out to serving your partners, vendors, and customers, and the world. It fundamentally requires that you serve without expecting anything in return—because it is the right thing to do. It means leading with passion and authenticity, and combining that with a purpose of doing good for others.

Practicing the spirit of vulnerability I discussed in Chapter Four, let's see how this servant-leadership approach to giving plays out inside Operation HOPE.

Most of our senior management team has been with us for more than ten years; and with the exception of our president and chief operating officer, Bill Walbrecher, who joined the firm two years ago when we created his position, all of the senior team has been with us for more than five years.

We do not pay the best salaries, give anyone signing bonuses, and of course as a nonprofit we don't have stock options. We don't have the best employee benefits package, although we continue to add value where we can. And until the last few years, we did not match investments in an employee retirement savings plan. So what is the "special sauce" that makes people stick around? The answer is this: a powerful combination of passion, authenticity, purpose, and servant leadership.

Even though I hope I am a fairly good boss today, I readily admit that I have been a far from perfect boss in the past. I can remember vividly how on so many occasions I simply did not handle stress or disappointment well. In fact, I was sometimes just plain bad.

In the early years of my career, I would often confuse a desire to get a job done with the real capacity for someone else to actually do the job. In other words, back then if people were not getting something accomplished, oftentimes it was either because I unreasonably expected them to be superhuman or because I was not giving them the time or the tools to achieve the task at hand.

My senior team stuck with me through those early years because they knew that when I blew up, although it was wholly inappropriate on my part, I was driven by my passion (a focus on the "we" of our work), and not a desire to be punitive (a focus on the "me" of my own selfish needs). Or as I told my assistant Debra Collins recently, when she asked me for advice as she prepared to give her second-ever speech in life: if you have passion and authenticity, the audience will forgive almost any other sin of delivery.

I believe that the people who work at Operation HOPE also knew instinctively that I was being an authentic servant leader, even when I was an absolutely crappy communicator. They knew I was not playing a game with them, the mission of our organization, or the people we served. Once they bought in to my authenticity, which you cannot fake, everything else always seemed to sort itself out.

Despite my immaturity as a leader early on, the vital mission and work of Operation HOPE was salvaged because we had an incredible overriding purpose: to serve our community. Our mission is to eradicate poverty as we know it and to spark a silver rights movement around the world through economic empowerment. We want to be involved in something larger and more important than ourselves, and want to believe that our lives make a difference. We want to have a purpose and serve. That is the special sauce that drives our organization, and it's what also drives the more than eight thousand HOPE Corps volunteers who are part of our growing silver rights movement around the world.

Today, because of that powerful sense of organizational purpose, aligned with competent and reliable management and driven by passion, authenticity, and a desire to do good, I find that my team is continually charged up to do more, even without my asking it of them. Far from being burned out, as is often the case with longtime people working in any organization, our team is more motivated today than at any time since the founding of HOPE.

In the rest of the chapter, we'll examine the two fundamental parts of the final law of leadership: first, that giving starts by giving to your people; and second, that giving must be done without expectations and instead with a purpose of doing good for others.

## GIVING TO YOUR PEOPLE

Giving starts with how you serve those who work inside your organization, and then radiates out to others you serve as part of your mission. How you treat your employees is an important sign of how you treat everyone else in your business and in your life. If you can get it right here, you can get it right with your customers, your clients, your stakeholders.

As the leader of your life, your family, your organization, your community, your city, or your country, you have got to represent the change you want to see in the world.

Love leadership of your people begins with love leadership inside of you. People have an incredible B.S. screen. They know when you are snowing them, and they know when you are being real.

Our team at Operation HOPE continually witnesses the boss working as hard or harder than they do to "get it right" for those we are chartered to serve. They see me crisscrossing the globe, meeting with leaders and potential new partners.

*They see me showing up.* Our staff sees me showing up

- In the offices of our partners around the world

- In the underserved communities we serve

- In our classrooms, regularly teaching a session on financial literacy or entrepreneurship

- At regular staff meetings, sitting in the back until I am asked to speak, *if* I am asked to speak

- Unannounced to work in our HOPE Center in Harlem or our HOPE Center outside of Washington, D.C., where I made sure the contractor built offices for me with my name on them, so that the community and our partners knew I came there regularly to work and meet with them whenever possible

They also see me showing up in the lives of our employees, and sometimes their families, too. If a family member passes away or one of our team members goes into the hospital, I show up at services or make a call to the hospital, as my traveling schedule allows. At the very least, I call on the phone or send a personal note.

If someone gets a promotion, everyone hears about it. And if someone leaves and has kept her promise to HOPE and the underserved communities we serve, I don't have someone else send her an impersonal e-mail and have HR collect her keys. We find a personal way of honoring her service, often by hosting an intimate gathering to chronicle her achievements with HOPE, honor her time here, and celebrate her contribution.

These ways of showing up do not take much effort, and they take even less money. But they do take interest. Little things count. Sometimes little things count the most. They're love leadership in action.

Today I show up with a simple question for our employees: "What can I do to help you do your job?" Most of the time the answer is, nothing at all, but staff members usually appreciate that I asked, and that I really listened when they responded. Employees know they have a chit of sorts in their pocket, if at a time in the future they have a need, or simply want to talk.

Employees want to know that their employer takes an interest in them for the long term and wants them to succeed. My friend Michael Critelli, former executive chairman and CEO of Pitney Bowes, a Fortune 500 company, recalls a lifetime achievement award his company gave to a twenty-eight-year sales executive. When this executive was asked the secret of his success, he answered, "It's very simple. I turn $30,000-a-year mailroom managers into successful $80,000-a-year VPs of administration."

Critelli says leadership boils down to making those who work for you successful. This salesperson made the assumption that every one of the people who worked for him wanted to feel successful in his or her own organizations, and he offered them solutions that made them successful. In return they offered him undying loyalty. He gave a lot; he received a lot.

Rachael Doff started as an intern at Operation HOPE, just a year after its founding; now, seventeen years later, she has risen through the ranks to become executive vice president and chief administrative officer, or the third most influential person in the organization. She shows how this approach has played out in her own life:

> I started a new job in the midst of mourning the end of a ten-year relationship. One summer day, I was struggling at work, and my new boss took me outside and sat with me on the steps in front of the office building. I will never forget that moment. He said, "You have given that person ten years of your life. Are you going to give them one more minute?" That statement was a turning point that set me on the road toward recovery. By loving me and investing in me, I am an employee and a friend for life. That person who loved me was, and is, John Hope Bryant.

Of course, I am in no way saying I do things perfectly, or that I always get things right with our people. Sometimes I blow it completely. But no one will tell you I don't try. You will not find anyone in this world who will tell you that John Hope Bryant consciously tried to hurt her. Someone might have gotten run over because she was standing in the wrong place at the wrong time and didn't hear me when I was coming through at a hundred miles an hour, on fire with mission, vision, passion, and purpose. But it was never conscious or intentional.

Intent matters when you are serving people. At Operation HOPE, our programs, products, and services boil down to our people. Without them, we are nothing. And without serving *them*, we won't achieve our ambitious goals.

## GIVING TO GET THE BEST OUT OF PEOPLE

Why does giving 100 percent plus to your employees matter? Because you are dealing with human beings and not human doings. People are not robots. With real people, you tend to get what you give. As Deepak Chopra wrote in *The Seven Spiritual Laws of Success*, "There is a perfect accounting system in this universe."[2] Whatever goes around, comes around.

When you give your employees the bare minimum, and demand that they respond to you because "you're the boss," of course they will comply. And *comply* is about all they will do. In Webster's dictionary, *compliance* is defined as "the act of conforming, acquiescing, or yielding. A tendency to yield readily to others, especially in a weak and subservient way."

The bare minimum is all you get from compliance, and no great enterprise was ever built on the bare minimum. You have to aspire to have an organization where people want to do more, to give of themselves, above the line of minimum expectations. That is where organizational greatness is found. You cannot buy this sort of commitment. You have to earn it.

This way of giving to your staff comes down to viewing the world as an optimist rather than as a pessimist. Leadership expert Bill George puts it this way:

> If people are in an environment that is very
> supportive to them, will they do a good job
> or will they slack off? And how you come to
> the answer to that question will determine the
> kind of leader you're going to be. If you believe
> people will slack off, then you're going to create
> a tight, rules-based environment where if people
> violate the rules, they're fired or forced out of the
> organization. If you believe that people who are
> in a positive reinforcing environment where they
> get lots of positive feedback for their good works
> are going to do better and the organization is
> going to be better, then you have a love-leadership
> organization.

Bill George is describing a decades-old tension between two competing theories of leadership. In the 1960s, Douglas McGregor at MIT's Sloan School of Management called them Theory X and Theory Y. The big difference between the two theories lies in how people are perceived, as McGregor explained in his book *The Human Side of Enterprise:*[3]

*Theory X*

- People are inherently lazy, and avoid work and responsibility whenever they can.

- People work only under conditions of external coercion and control, which is the manager's job to provide.

- People are only out for themselves and won't work without incentives or the threat of punishment.

- People know less about their jobs than their supervisors do.

*Theory Y*

- People may be hardworking, self-directed, and responsible in meeting their goals, if they are committed to those goals.

- People are more productive without rigid rules and procedures.

- People are inherently motivated when work meets some of their higher-order needs, such as the need for self-fulfillment or the satisfaction of doing a good job.

- People usually know more about their jobs than their supervisors do.

Theory Y, therefore, calls for decentralizing power and delegating authority. It advocates broadening the scope of employees' jobs, to give them more variety and boost their self-esteem. It endorses consulting employees about decisions, so as to tap the power of their intelligence and heighten their sense of control over their own lives.

Theory Y supports with elegant simplicity the fifth law that I am proposing in this book: giving is getting. It simply pays dividends to invest in the people who are investing in you.

Explains Frank Krings, chief operating officer of Hypo Real Estate Holding, also a YGL, and formerly Deutsche Bank's COO Europe:

We're not infinitely capable. There are limits to what you can achieve by yourself. If I get known for having better teams, that's where I am successful. Maybe I'm selfish, because I like to have good teams around me and to develop a track record of creating sustainable and successful teams.

If you try to do that the command-and-control way, you're going to lose the battle on day one. Ultimately what you do is align. You show employees how you behave and how you want them to behave; you give them the sense that you don't interfere with what's important to them; you explain the rules of the game and the territory in which they can operate, and then empower them to be competitive within that environment. That's not only a successful model, it's a necessary model.

There's another critical way you get people to give their best: you help them find and follow their passion.

In the past, Mary Hagerty, who is now my global chief of financial literacy, did three jobs at one time: fund development, accounting, and real estate development. She accomplished the building of our first HOPE Center in South Central Los Angeles, but her strengths were simply not in fund development or accounting.

Mary never complained about anything, but one day she told me, "John, if you actually put me in a job I am passionate about, and try to make it just one job, I will actually excel at it." I did, and she has. Mary has today educated more than 380,000 youth globally through our award-winning Banking on Our Future financial literacy program.

And then there's Lance Triggs, who came to HOPE with no experience in financial services. But as soon as we allowed him to focus on what he was passionate about within the HOPE family, which was adult economic empowerment, he too excelled. Today Lance is executive vice president and chief of the HOPE Banking Center network nationally. Under his leadership, individuals enrolled in our credit-counseling program have increased their credit scores on average from 570 (the predatory lending range) to 650 (the mainstream banking services range) in only eighteen months. Lance has also created hundreds of new first-time home owners who have not faced foreclosure, and helped thousands of home owners avoid foreclosure through our Mortgage HOPE Crisis Hotline.

Both of these individuals found an organization that was passionate about them and then allowed them to figure out what *they* were passionate about. That's love leadership in action.

Jim Clifton is chairman and CEO of the Gallup Organization, and definitely falls in the category of a love leader. Over the past decade, Gallup has surveyed more than ten million people worldwide on the topic of employee engagement. Only one-third "strongly agree" with the statement, "At work, I have the opportunity to do what I do best every day." And for those who do not get to focus on what they do best—their strengths—the costs are staggering. In a recent poll of more than a thousand people, among those who "strongly disagree" or "disagreed" with this "what I do best" statement, *not one single person* was emotionally engaged on the job.

In contrast, Gallup has found that people who do have the opportunity to focus on their strengths every day are six times as likely to be engaged in their jobs and more than three times as likely to report having an excellent quality of life in general. That's love leadership in action, too.

## GIVING, NOT TAKING

The opposite of giving and serving is taking. It is the Theory X brand of pessimism. If you're a taker in life, you're sliding down a slippery slope. You go from taking emotionally from those you love to forgetting who you are and taking whatever you want. And that kind of lifestyle can too easily descend into illegal and unethical behavior.

My point is that when you're a taker, your universe just gets smaller. You're not building an environment of trust, you're not building character, you're not building a group of investors in what you believe. No one likes you or trusts you.

And like any addiction, taking requires more tomorrow than it did today to give you the same return. If you're an alcoholic, you need more alcohol tomorrow to give you the same buzz you had yesterday. If you're a drug addict, you start off casually with one hit a month, then one a week, and after a while, you're getting high four or five times a day. You're trying to fill a cup that doesn't have a bottom. Unless you deal with the real problem, ultimately you will just kill yourself.

To be a taker is expensive. If you are the sort of manager who takes, the only way you motivate your people is by paying them off. You have to give them more tomorrow than you gave them yesterday for the same outcome. Eventually they're not satisfied with just getting more money and things. They ultimately want your job, so they conspire against you.

Says the Reverend Murray:

True giving has no expectation except to be allowed to deliver, leaving the packet on the doorstop even if the other person will not answer the doorbell. But then, giver, you arrive at home, and in your mailbox is a surprise of surprises. You have just won a jackpot. What goes around, comes around.

In the marketplace, you become known as a giver. Down the hallway in a corner office is a known taker. You know from observation that takers are not going away. It's just that they are short lived, and then another taker fills the void. The question is, Is that who you are? Of course not.

And the same way you can see it, others can see it. You love. You care. You give. You do not tremble or be troubled by those who advance by taking. You are in control of yourself—asking nothing and giving everything. When the dust clears, you will be left standing.

Human beings are naturally good. We learn bad. It was the great author and theologian C. S. Lewis who said that even badness is nothing more than "spoiled goodness."

A good business plan is the opposite of taking. Good capitalism, as I call it, means to have an open hand, not a closed fist. It involves building a group of people who believe in you and your vision, who trust you, whom you don't have to buy off or coerce.

If you want to have a prosperous, sustainable life, you'll find it cheaper, smarter, and easier to do the work of love leadership. You will be better off in the long term if you inspire people, get them to believe in your vision, invest in them so they trust you, reward good behavior, build relationships. People will do the work they're inspired to do rather than the work that you force them to do.

When you give, it's like throwing a pebble in a lake. There's a ripple effect as other people sign on to your vision.

This plays out every day for Operation HOPE. If we don't have people talking about our work positively all around the world and wanting to support our vision in hard times, we're dead. If we don't have goodwill built up over years of giving, we're finished. In a pure business context, you would call this reputation or brand management.

During this difficult period that began in 2008, Operation HOPE has needed to get a little bit. I've had to call on relationships with our supporters to ask for their help, even while they are saying no to others, and at a time when they are having to restructure and lay off people. And everyone I've called has been helpful. I haven't had one person tell me no. They haven't always given me the answers I wanted, but they've given me the best answer they can give me.

That is a result of relationships. That is the result of my giving to them over a long period of time. The dividend paid on that relationship is that now, when I need it, our supporters are there for us. And that's probably why we have been able to make it through this crisis so far without having to lay off employees or close an office.

I may have to get to that point, but I'm proud that we've come this far without having to take that step. I'm convinced it's because we have made a business out of giving, not taking.

## DOING GOOD FOR OTHERS PAYS OFF

The fifth law of love leadership, giving is getting, means not only leading with authenticity and in service to your people but also leading with the purpose of doing good for others.

When you think about it, life is made up of little moments that most of us never notice or acknowledge. When I go through the doors at the airport, for instance, I'll intentionally wait and hold the door for the guy behind me. And almost every time, as soon as I hold the door for him, he'll turn around and hold the door for the person behind him.

Another way to describe this principle is *pay it forward*. I give someone something he doesn't deserve. He then turns around and gives someone else something she doesn't deserve. The world's a better place as a result.

Darys Estrella Mordan knows the power of paying it forward. She grew up in the small mountain town of San Jose de Ocoa in the Dominican Republic. When Hurricane David destroyed her hometown in 1979, her family moved to Santo Domingo, the capital, where she attended Catholic school and graduated at the top of her class. She then moved to New York and lived with an aunt in Queens.

She studied English on tape and enrolled at LaGuardia Community College, then transferred to Vassar College. After graduation, she worked for a hedge fund, then earned an MBA from the University of Michigan, going on to work at Goldman Sachs, where she rose to the position of vice president. In 2007, she was recruited to become the CEO of the Bolsa de Valores, the Dominican Republic's capital markets exchange—the first woman ever to have held such a position in Latin America.[4]

When I talk to kids I tell them, "You don't need to give me anything in return because I'm fine, thank God. You need to do the same for others, and that's what's going to make the world a better place." If I can practice that every day of my life, I'm a happy person. And if I could influence one kid out of four thousand when I speak to them, I did my job.

Jerry Jurgensen embodies the principle of servant leadership more than any CEO I know. He has a lot to share about being the leader of Nationwide, the insurance powerhouse, but all he wanted to talk about during a recent interview was service and doing good for others. These days, Jurgensen spends a lot of time trying to reform education. He learned the concept of service in his Jesuit high school in Omaha, Nebraska:

> We were taught and reminded every single day that we were put on the planet for others. We were told, "Some of you will hit life's lottery; some of you won't. It won't all be a function of how smart you are."

> I have learned that success happens at the intersection of luck, fate, gifts, and skill. But it's an intersection. And the fast lanes to the intersection are luck and fate.

> In the end, there will be a day of judgment, and we're only going to get asked about one thing. Somebody's going to look at us and say: "Tell me what you did down there. Did you leave it better than you found it?"

Doing good is deeply personal to civil rights icon Andrew Young—our nation's first African American ambassador to the United Nations, the closest aide to Rev. Dr. Martin Luther King during the civil rights movement, and my personal hero in life. I recently asked Young why he gives away more than half the money he makes each year. I remember what he told me as if it were yesterday:

> We made $6,000 a year during the civil rights movement with Dr. King, and I was honored to do it. But today I get paid tens of thousands of dollars, and have had untold opportunity in my life, in large part because my friend Dr. King gave his life. It is not my money. We are stewards of this money, but it really is not ours. I also believe that the more you get, the more you give, and it comes back to you tenfold.

And true to form, Young's formula for giving has worked like a charm. Back when he was mayor of Atlanta in the 1980s, he made about $50,000 a year. He was an honest mayor, so that meant he really did make only $50,000 a year.

At the time, his church approached him to serve as chairman for a giving campaign to raise $500,000; the church leadership thought he would be perfect for the assignment, given his global name and recognition. The only problem was that the church elders wanted him, as chairman, to make the lead gift of $50,000, an impossible thing for someone who only made that same amount in a year.

Young went home and told his wife, Jean Childs Young, since deceased, "We can't do this. It is our annual income, and we cannot afford it."

"Andy, where would we be without the church?" Jean responded. "The church led you to Dr. King. The church brought us together. We have to do this. The Lord will make a way."

"Well, he better," Young responded, almost without considering what Jean had just said.

Young made that $50,000 commitment to the church, and a short time later when he was making his way through the Atlanta airport, a man approached him. "Mr. Young, Mr. Young," the man called out. "I am a publisher, and I would love it if you would consider writing a book for me on religion."

Young responded that he would prefer to write his own book about the civil rights movement. The publisher refused to let up, saying, "If you would just write a book on religion first, then you can write on civil rights or anything else you want."

Young shrugged his shoulders in his classic, easygoing fashion, saying, "Sure, I will consider it. Here is the number of my agent in New York. I guess you can call him if you are interested."

About a week later, Young got a call from his agent, who said, "Did you agree to write a book recently?"

"I guess," responded Young.

"Well, I have a contract here for you in duplicate," his agent continued. "It looks OK to me. Why don't you sign it and keep one copy." And then, almost as an afterthought, his agent added, "They will be sending you an advance check for $50,000."

When Andrew Young got that check, he endorsed it and handed it straight over to his church. He believes he never would have gotten that money, and the opportunity to write several books, if it were not for his commitment to give to his church. Needless to say, he has since made multiples of that initial amount on the books he subsequently wrote for this publisher, and he also served on the company's board of directors for ten years, earning more than $75,000 a year in board fees alone.

*The more you give, the more you get* is the literal truth. Or as Quincy Jones learned from growing up during the Depression, "Empty the cup every time, so it comes back twice as full. Because if you give everything you've got, it comes back twofold."

David L. Brewer III, former superintendent of the Los Angeles Unified School District, agrees that you always receive more than you give:

Good things happen to those who give. But you can't give selfishly. I always distinguish between giving and investing. Some people give unselfishly. But some people invest. And sometimes you can get that message confused, because when you invest, what do you expect? You expect a return. If you give, you don't expect a return.

Although he does not expect it, David Lizárraga sees a return on giving every day as president and CEO of TELACU. With $120 million in revenues, TELACU is the largest community development corporation in the United States, and works to improve the lives of people through service, empowerment, advancement, and the creation of self-sufficiency. It is a nonprofit that operates a family of for-profit companies that serve primarily the Latino community and have a double bottom line—profit-ability that is inseparable from social impact. TELACU gives back with a significant reinvestment of its profits into community programs that serve college students, seniors, and at-risk youth.

Lizárraga says that giving comes from a spirit of love and service:

> Love can conquer all. You give from the standpoint of being of service and loving to be of service, and loving the people who you're serving, whatever condition they may be in. It gives you a way of being that doesn't accept failure. Because love is not selfish. It's not about "What can I get?" but

"What can I give?" It's not about deeds. It's about results. It's about sacrifice.

## WHY YOU GIVE: GOOD SELFISHNESS

Lizárraga and Brewer make an important point about selfishness. But here I'll take a position that's slightly different from that of my good friends.

Let's make this plain: giving is also in your own enlightened self-interest. I call the concept *good selfishness*. When you want to help others, they want to help you. When you want to do good, the universe wants you to do well. But if you want to use people, they will feel used. It's all about intent.

Intent matters. That's why I don't say "self-interest"; I say "enlightened self-interest." I don't say "selfishness"; I say "good selfishness." I don't say "capitalism"; I say "good capitalism." The intent is to do good.

Former president Bill Clinton explains it this way:

The act of giving is an example of good selfishness because it will almost always make you feel good, or in the case of businesses, it will result in positive things for your bottom line. I think the work of my foundation is a wonderful example of this. We now have 1.4 million people accessing AIDS medicines under agreements that we've negotiated with dozens of pharmaceutical companies—but the companies that give us this medicine make money. We insist that they do. They just make money in a different way. Instead of making a higher margin on a lower volume, they make money selling a higher volume with a lower margin, and they keep more people alive. We try to show people and companies that doing good and doing well can be one and the same. In the end, the wise person comes to understand that selfishness and enlightened selfishness are one and the same.

The fourteenth-century German philosopher Heinrich Seuse says that your quality of life is closely linked to your ethics in life. In other words, when you make ethically sound decisions, you actually improve your life quality.

Or as Prince Haakon of Norway put it to me, "When you grant someone else dignity and lift them, that's when you feel better yourself. You actually increase your own dignity." The heir to the Norwegian throne lives a life of privilege, and he rides around the world's capitals in a motorcade that rivals that of any head of state. But he's motivated in life by giving.

HRH Prince Jaime de Bourbon-Parma is another member of royalty whose history of giving and social responsibility goes back a long way. Bourbon-Parma is a member of the extended Dutch royal family, and currently works as a Dutch diplomat who has served in Iraq and Afghanistan. He has fond memories of his grandfather, who died when the prince was young. His grandfather knew war for most of his life. He fought in World War I, the Spanish Civil War, and World War II, when he joined the French Resistance and consequently ended up as a prisoner in the concentration camps in Natzweiler and Dachau, Germany.

My grandfather survived the concentration camps. He did not choose to survive by taking, for instance the little food there was, from others. Instead, he would sit with prisoners and talk to them about the meaning of life. For one person, he wanted to survive to see his wife and children. For the next it was because he wanted to finish his life work. For another his faith gave him strength.

Everybody has something that makes them tick, in the most horrible circumstances, something to help rebuild their lives. And he reminded them of it so there would be no despair. You needed to be mentally strong to have a chance of surviving the concentration camps. For my grandfather, giving to others gave him strength to survive.

Proventus CEO Daniel Sachs agrees, but puts it slightly differently.

There's a lot of talk of responsibility and of ethics. All those things are good, and I respect and cherish those values. But I think we need to get back to a discussion about self-interest. I have to contribute to building a better society because it's good for all of us, and it's good for me, as well.

We're all selfish, and we're all imperfect. I agree with Bishop Ulmer that a saint is a sinner who got up. We're bums sometimes, but we're trying to be good people. Trying to be good is the intent. That's the amazing part. We don't love *because of*, we love *in spite of*—in spite of the fact that we do stupid things.

And why should you love someone else in spite of? Because you're loved in spite of. Don't assume that because you're not Nelson Mandela, you can't do good. Don't assume that because you don't have the wisdom of Rev. Dr. Martin Luther King, you've got to be a bum. Don't assume that because you can't be Mahatma Gandhi, you've got to be a robber baron. We shouldn't leave saving the world to saints, and we shouldn't leave capitalism to sinners.

Why don't you accept your humanness and admit that you're imperfect and you make mistakes, but that you're trying to be the best person you can be? What we truly want to practice is good selfishness. Don't be ashamed to admit that you want to benefit. But you want others to benefit *more*.

Admit that you like raising your children. You like seeing them grow up, you like seeing them excel, you like helping them with their problems. These things make you feel good.

Admit that you like running that nonprofit. It helps you feel that you're making a difference and changing the world.

Admit that you like nurturing and mentoring your employees. It makes you feel that your life has meaning and that you're not just working to pay your bills. You're giving more than you're getting, and your life will leave a legacy.

Admit that volunteering makes you feel good. You feel that your life, what you've learned, and what you have to give are valuable to someone else. You're seeing that person's life transformed because of you.

Let's admit that we're selfish. And then we should differentiate that feeling from bad selfishness. Our purpose is love, is giving, is goodness, is service. To quote my friend and political hero former president Bill Clinton from his best-selling book *Giving,* "It just makes you feel good."

# CONCLUSION:
# GOOD CAPITALISM AND
# LOVE LEADERSHIP

Today the world faces a need for love leadership that is greater and more urgent than at any time in history.

As I am writing this book, it is estimated that by the end of our current financial crisis, more than $2 trillion in asset value will have fallen off the balance sheets of some of the largest and most sophisticated financial institutions in the world, and there will be an estimated $20 trillion reduction in private wealth in the United States alone. So far, among developed economies, the United States and the United Kingdom have reported record foreclosure rates on home mortgages. More than one million homes have been left unoccupied in the United States alone. Auto sales have plunged. Companies have been laying off employees and going bankrupt at a blistering pace.

In many ways, our present situation is a wakeup call for America. To quote John C. Mellott, the former longtime publisher of the *Atlanta Journal-Constitution*, we are living through a "crisis of virtues." Our habits of moral goodness have eroded. And we are all to blame.

After the riots of 1992 in Los Angeles, I ran into a wall of indifference that is at the heart of this crisis of virtues. The long-term response to this tragedy was not, as I had hoped, an increased effort in healing and building community; instead, we witnessed a growing collection of private gated communities, private schools, private cars, and private jets. Everyone went back to his or her life of instant gratification and the day-to-day business of "getting" and asking "What's in it for me?" As a friend said to me, "indifference is the death knell of the soul."

If this crisis causes all of us to take a new look at our lives and how we are living them, and to reassess what is really important and how we are all interconnected, then in the end the crisis may be a good thing. As I keep saying, this is not so much a recession as a reset.

## WE NEED GOOD SELFISHNESS AND GLOBAL GOOD CAPITALISM

When we look closely at how we got here, it's easy to point a finger at our economic system. I still believe that capitalism works. In fact, I would go further and say that nothing has done more to lift the world's poor out of poverty than market-based economics. But the current economic model is broken, and what has been done to the system has given business a bad name.

Of late, there has been increasing criticism of our basic economic model. But what has been going on is not so much capitalism as bad capitalism. Bad capitalism is a result of an obsessive focus on a fairly narrow band of short-term financial results. The aim is to make money, to the exclusion of all other considerations. In this context, I believe that the major financial rating agencies need to take another look at their formula for defining "shareholder value," because as we have seen, the answer is not merely short-term financial gain.

I argue that the problem with business today is not capitalism itself, but rather its abuse. Short-termism, greed, laziness, and selfishness have grown rampant. All these things are first cousins to fear, as we saw earlier in this book. As someone noted, in the past we suffered from irrational exuberance. Well, now we suffer from irrational fear, and in the end, fear fails.

In Chapter Five I made the point that bad selfishness is where I benefit but everyone else pays a price for it, and good selfishness is where I benefit but everyone else benefits more. History has shown that capitalism succeeds when it practices good selfishness. The system succeeds when it practices *good capitalism*.

Madam C. J. Walker became the first black millionaire in America because she worked hard and provided a source of economic empowerment for the thousands of women who made good money selling her line of beauty products. She was passionate about teaching women and minorities a trade during the postslavery era. Ultimately she built the largest business owned by an African American, male or female, up to that time. She amassed a fortune that she largely gave away, and left a legacy of service, hope, self-esteem, opportunity, and entrepreneurship for the black community.

Entrepreneurs like Walker became rich along the way, but they also created a vision, empowered people, added value, and built a long-term agenda. It wasn't about the money. They liked the money, I am sure, and they loved the lifestyle comforts it brought, but their principal pursuit in life was not the money. They wanted to give. They understood the difference between making money and building real wealth, just as they saw the difference between treating their clients as cogs in a transaction and treating them as equal partners in a relationship. They were love-based leaders.

What I am advocating is an enlightened model of good capitalism, good selfishness, and what my hero Andrew Young calls "free enterprise for the people" in the twenty-first century. We should want all boats to rise, not just the yachts.

Why should we care about how someone less fortunate does? The short answer is that caring for the success and prosperity of others, particularly those at the bottom rungs of the success ladder, is the only way, over the long term, that those who are well off are ever going to be able to keep the precious wealth that they have been able to accumulate.

Gated communities will not save anyone. The only thing that can save us all is hope made real in people's lives. The most dangerous person alive is a person without hope.

In a city like Los Angeles, with more than six million people "protected" by around ten thousand police officers, security is an illusion at best. The reality is that people stop at red lights, go to school, pay their parking tickets, and obey the law because they believe. They believe that if they work hard, play by the rules, and do the right thing, they will be rewarded with an opportunity to succeed or fail on their own merits.

With hope, anything is possible. Prosperity is the partner of peace. But without hope, when people don't believe in the future and don't value their own life or others, there is simply not enough law enforcement available in the world to maintain order.

## A CALL TO ACTION

We are called today to do more than we have ever done in the past to rebuild this nation and help it once again achieve the greatness that is its potential. In this important work, there's much we can learn from love-based leaders who've faced situations as monumental in the past.

Dorothy Height is a legendary civil rights activist, pathbreaking president of the National Council of Negro Women, and recipient of the Congressional Gold Medal, the nation's highest civilian honor. The ninety-six-year-old leader has the unique distinction of being an adviser to every president since Franklin Delano Roosevelt. She was on stage with the Reverend Dr. Martin Luther King when he gave his "I Have a Dream" speech.

In her struggles on behalf of civil rights and against America's pernicious legacy of racial violence and discrimination, Height has seen the power of moving with long-term determination, one step at a time. You do one thing, which makes it possible for others to come after you and push that work further. "We have to do whatever we can in our time, while we're still here," she said to me recently.

I had the good fortune to hear what Height has learned about leadership in tough times. She told me that leadership is about more than being in charge:

> Leadership is the willingness and capacity to respond to what is needed in a situation. And many of us have that opportunity to give leadership. You may be in a group of twenty people, and you know something needs to be done. You may not be the leader, but you're going to give leadership to the group by responding in some way that you help it to move. You can open the gate for others to come in.
>
> I think leadership helps to release people. Many people are much more than they think they are, but they need someone to help them realize themselves. And once those people begin to move

together and work together, they release new
energy and new possibility within themselves.

She remembers a meeting in 1946 where she and
other leaders in the national YWCA were attempting to
get the organization to pass its interracial charter for full
integration of every YWCA in the nation, which eventually passed. Some white leaders in attendance left, refus-
ing even to stay to discuss the proposal. To this day she
remembers the response of Dr. Benjamin Elijah Mays,
former president of Morehouse College and the man
whom Dr. King called his "spiritual mentor." She remembers Dr. Mays saying, "I'm sure some of you say the time
is not right, but if you have a Christian purpose, then it's
your job to ripen the time."

"That's the kind of spirit that it takes," Height said to
me. "You can't just keep saying that the time isn't ready
for this."

The time is ripe for all of us to reassert the power of
good capitalism. We must all become what Dr. Height calls
"dreamers, with shovels in our hands." With the power of
good capitalism—and the principles of love leadership—
behind us, we can overcome the global crisis.

In the increasingly interconnected world we live
in, when one person succeeds, we all succeed. And con-
versely, when one fails, we all fail.

As we move to restructure our global economy, we
need to make sure that the conversation is based on a

love-leadership model, has a long-range vision, and empowers people to participate and to become legitimate stakeholders in the system.

Rainbows after storms. Never let a good crisis go to waste.

Let's use this crisis as an opportunity to make our world great again. We can launch a movement that finally makes capitalism work for us all. We can launch a global movement of love leadership.

Hope is on the way.

# LIST OF INTERVIEWEES

These are the thirty love-based leaders interviewed for this book:

Shai Agassi, founder and chief executive officer, Better Place

HRH Jaime Bernardo, Prince de Bourbon-Parma, Count of Bardi

David Brewer III, former superintendent of schools, Los Angeles Unified School District

Hon. William Jefferson Clinton, former president of the United States

Michael Critelli, chairman and chief executive officer (retired), Pitney Bowes, Inc.

William George, professor of management practice, Harvard Business School

HRH Crown Prince Haakon Magnus of Norway

Mary L. Hagerty, first senior vice president, chief of global
financial literacy initiatives, Operation HOPE, Inc.

George Haligowski, chairman and chief executive officer,
ITLA Capital/Imperial Capital Bank

William Hanna, managing director, Jacobs Capital Group,
LLC

Richard Hartnack, vice chairman, US Bancorp

Cara Heiden, copresident, Wells Fargo Home Mortgage

Dr. Dorothy Height, chair and president emeritus,
National Council for Negro Women, Inc.

Quincy Jones, chairman and chief executive officer,
Quincy Jones Productions

Jerry Jurgensen, former chief executive officer, Nationwide

Secretary Jack Kemp, founder and chairman, Kemp
Partners, recently deceased

Richard Kovacevich, chairman, Wells Fargo

Frank Krings, chief operating officer, member of the
board, Hypo Real Estate Holding AG

David Lizárraga, president and chief executive officer,
TELACU

Leslie Maasdorp, vice chairman, Barclays Capital

Rod McGrew, president and chief executive officer, Love
& Happiness Productions

Thomas McInerney, chairman and chief executive officer,
ING Americas

Rodrigo Hübner Mendes, founder, Instituto Rodrigo
Mendes

Darys Estrella Mordan, chief executive officer, Dominican
    Republic Stock Exchange
Lynn Pike, president, Capital One Banking Business
Álvaro Rodríguez Arregui, chief financial officer, Vitro;
    chairman, ACCIÓN International; cofounder and
    managing partner, Ignia
Daniel Sachs, chief executive officer, Proventus AB
Zainab Salbi, president and chief executive officer, Women
    for Women International
Lance W. Triggs, executive vice president, HOPE Banking
    Center Network, Operation HOPE, Inc.
Ambassador Andrew Young, chairman, GoodWorks
    International, LLC

# NOTES

CHAPTER TWO

1. Kate Kelly and Merissa Marr, "Boss-Zilla!" *Wall Street Journal*, September 24, 2005, http://online.wsj.com/article/SB112749746571150033.html.

2. Emily Gould, "New York's Worst Bosses," Gawker.com, March 13, 2007, http://gawker.com/news/evil-bosses/new-yorks-worst-bosses-scott-rudin-243908.php.

3. Gould, "New York's Worst Bosses."

4. Workplace Bullying Institute, "U.S. Workplace Bullying Survey," September 2007, http://bullyinginstitute.org/zogby2007/wbi-zogby2007.html.

5. Loraleigh Keashly and Karen Jagatic, "The Nature, Extent, and Impact of Emotional Abuse in the Workplace: Results of a Statewide Survey" (paper, Academy of Management conference, Toronto, August 8, 2000).

6. Niccolò Machiavelli, *The Prince and Other Political Writings*, trans. Stephen J. Milner (London: Everyman Paperbacks, 1995).

7. Andrew Ross Sorkin, "Rating Agencies Draw Fire on Capitol Hill," *New York Times*, October 22, 2008, http://dealbook.blogs.nytimes.com/2008/10/22/rating-agencies-draw-fire-capitol-hill/?scp=1&sq=ratings%20agency%20cows&st=cse.

CHAPTER FIVE

1. Robert K. Greenleaf, *Servant Leadership* (New York: Paulist Press, 1977).

2. Deepak Chopra, *The Seven Spiritual Laws of Success* (San Rafael, Calif.: Amber-Allen Publishing, 1994).

3. Andrea Gabor, *The Capitalist Philosophers* (New York: Times Books, 2000), 153–185.

4. Heather Appel, "Home Economics: Darys Estrella Mordan '92 Shaping Her Country's Financial Future," *Vassar,* Winter 2007, http://www.aavc.vassar.edu/vq/articles/features-winter07 -mordan.

# ACKNOWLEDGMENTS

Writing this book was a true labor of love for me, and a number of pretty amazing individuals had to do a lot of work in both supporting me and putting up with me as I worked through the process of getting my vision, spirit, and really my life mission statement down on paper. I'd like to thank my Operation HOPE board, employee, and HOPE Corps volunteer family, in particular my board vice chairman and friend, Tim Chrisman; my indispensible personal chief of staff, Rachael Doff, who has been tolerating me for sixteen years now; as well as my executive assistants, Leslie Alessandro and Debra Collins. And to the other key members of my senior management team, including Bill Walbrecher, Frederick D. Smith, Jena Roscoe, Emily Ausbrook, Rochelle Zawodny, Sharon Jones, Norbert Horvath, Ilya Monroe, Evelyn Ducoulombier, Juana Alba Rosales, and Maxine Brooks, thank you. A thank-you goes out to my friends who read sections of this book along the way and who also gave me their honest feedback, including my angelic mother-in-law Mrs. Janie Sykes Kennedy, best friend Rod McGrew, Ms. Naheed Elyasi and Ms. Sherry John, and Professor Pekka Himanen, my fellow Young Global Leader.

Others who provided important support to me through the process of book publishing included David Ratner of Newman Communications; Stacy Tisdale, coauthor of *The True Cost of Happiness;* writer Cameron Stauth; my amazing agent, Pilar Queen (or "Queen Pilar," as I like to call her); former president Bill Clinton's right arm, or "body man" as I like to refer to him, Doug Band; Sharon Harkey of Purple Shark Transcriptions; and all my inspiring friends at the World Economic Forum, the Forum of Young Global Leaders, the William Jefferson Clinton Foundation, and the Clinton Global Initiatives.

Part of my inspiration for this book is attributed to individuals currently in public service, from both sides of the political aisle, who continue to "do the right thing" even as the perversion of influence, power, and position that is Washington, D.C., politics constantly seems to pull them in another direction: Anna Cabral (former U.S. treasurer), Barry Jackson (former assistant to the president for strategic initiatives and external affairs), and Julie Cram (deputy assistant to the president and director of public liaison), all of whom served during the Bush administration; my friends in the House, particularly the brilliant and caring Congresswoman Dianne E. Watson

(D-CA) and Congresswoman Sheila Jackson-Lee (D-TX); former federal reserve vice chairman Preston Martin, who used his influence and relationships to introduce me to the Federal Reserve system, later donating along with his wife Genevieve $1 million to Operation HOPE (both now deceased); former federal reserve chairman Alan Greenspan; federal reserve chairman Ben Bernanke; U.S. comptroller John Dugan; and the Honorable Sheila Bair, who in my estimation is the best FDIC chair in the history of the agency. Thank you also to Charles Schwab, chairman of the U.S. President's Advisory Council on Financial Literacy, supported by Carrie Schwab-Pomerantz and Michael Townsend, for putting up with me while we work together to make financial literacy a reality for all Americans. My deep appreciation also goes to the only wise man I have ever known, my play father, the Reverend Dr. Cecil "Chip" Murray, who basically raised me in my adult life; to Pastor Charles E. Blake, presiding bishop for the six-million-strong Church of God in Christ and a true servant leader in the ministry, who inspires me to be a "better" person and leader; and to South African Archbishop-Emeritus Desmond Tutu, who instructs us all that religion is like a knife: it can be used to butter a slice of bread for the homeless or to cut the arm off of our brother. Our choice.

I'm also grateful to the leaders who shared their stories and their unique point of view of love leadership with me for this book. I could not fit all of the interviews, such as those with Shelley Freeman, Joseph S. Nye Jr., Michael Krause, Aaron McCormack, Andrew Cohen, John Osborne, Carole Wainaina, Caroline Casey, and others, nor all of these leaders' great stories, between the covers of this book, but you can still access many of the full interviews and stories from these amazing leaders at www.bryantgroup companies.com. A big thanks to Rebecca Browning, who saw the potential of the book from the beginning; to my amazing "crack that whip" editor, Genoveva Llosa; and to the entire, passionate Jossey-Bass team, especially Byron Schneider, Mary Garrett, Gayle Mak, Erin Moy, Amy Packard, Adrian Morgan, Nick Snider, and Cedric Crocker. What a class act you all are. Thanks for never letting me be mediocre.

I am grateful to Professor Klaus Schwab, founder and chairman of the World Economic Forum as well as the Forum of Young Global Leaders, for drilling into my head that we are all "global citizens" and for introducing me to my second, global family—the more than eight hundred members of Young Global Leaders (YGL). Special thanks to WEF staff David Aikman, Martina Gmur, and Marie France Roger for sharing valuable insights and enriching my experience as a YGL. What an amazing group of inspiring future leaders, and in many ways the inspiration for me to write this book, in particular Zainab Salbi and Shai Agassi. It was YGL that introduced me to the great Bill George, whom along with his wife, Penny, I treasure as new and important friends. You see, Bill and Penny's foundation helped sponsor the Kennedy School of Government "global leadership and public policy" program I completed at Harvard University in 2008. Believing that life and leadership are about making and keeping commitments, yes, but also about "showing up," Bill actually taught the closing session at Harvard, which I think was one of the best leadership experiences I have ever had.

Likewise, Sean Cleary, a senior adviser to the chairman at the World Economic Forum, helped me see a world beyond my experience and perspective; together with Mayor Herman Bailey, Sean is also the reason Operation HOPE is now in South Africa. He recently traveled from South Africa to the United States, at his own expense, to speak at the HOPE board retreat in California. Sean, whom I call the "South African James Bond," one of the people who helped craft the South African constitution, lives his life centered in the belief that giving is the receiving. Any search of his name will confirm that this approach of "giving is getting" has paid and continues to pay enormous dividends to him.

A very special personal thank-you to my family, including my mother, Juanita Smith; my father, Johnnie W. Smith; my sisters, Mara Lamont Hoskins and Arlene Hayes; my brother, Dave D. Harris, and his family; my goddaughters, Kirstin Fouché and Jade Howard; my brother- and sister-in-law James Kennedy and Dr. Teresa "Kay-Aba" Kennedy; and of course "my sweetie," Mrs. Sheila Kennedy Bryant, the *ultimate love leader* and truly the nicest, kindest person I know. Thanks for putting up with me and doing without me throughout the multiple evenings and weekends I spent trying to get this book right. Of course, I cannot leave out the true king of the Bryant household: our Yorkshire terrier, Little Man. Talk about love—I still marvel at how moments after disciplining Little Man, he has crawled back into my lap, giving me love I did not think I deserved. If only human beings treated each other half as kindly.

Finally and most of all, I want to take a moment to thank someone who was an indispensable part of getting this book exactly right, and that is Mickey Butts. Mickey was there throughout the development of the book, and I cannot give him enough credit for his superior eye, his command of research, his ability to take all of my energy and passion and organize it into a coherent thought process, and most of all for helping me get my "voice" on paper. I could not have asked for a better collaborator than Mickey Butts.

# ABOUT THE AUTHOR

**John Hope Bryant** is a philanthropic entrepreneur and businessman, in the business of empowerment. Raised in Compton and South Central Los Angeles, California, today he travels the world, tirelessly promoting a sense of hope, self-esteem, dignity, and opportunity for the underserved.

He is the founder, chairman, and chief executive officer of Operation HOPE, America's first nonprofit social investment banking organization, now operating in sixty-eight U.S. communities and in South Africa. Working with HOPE global spokesman Ambassador Andrew Young, Bryant is also a leader for a new movement bridging civil rights to silver rights. In 2008, Bryant was appointed by President George W. Bush as vice chairman of the bipartisan U.S. President's Advisory Council on Financial Literacy and now proudly serves the historic presidency of the Honorable Barack Obama, forty-fourth president of

the United States. In this role, Bryant is also chairman
of the Under-Served Committee for the U.S. President's
Council.

He was selected as a Young Global Leader for the
World Economic Forum, where he currently serves on the
Global Agenda Council as an adviser on financial literacy
and financial empowerment. As a cofounder of Global
Dignity, an affiliate of the Forum of Young Global Leaders
and the HOPE Global Initiative, he has conducted a
teaching session on dignity—*Dignity Day*—to youth and
leaders in Canada, Turkey, India, Switzerland, Finland,
South Africa, and Jordan, among other countries.

Bryant has also served on several corporate boards; is
a former goodwill ambassador to the United States for the
United Nations in Geneva, Switzerland; and is a partner
with former president Bill Clinton and his foundation,
teaching financial literacy and promoting the Earned
Income Tax Credit.

An internationally respected public speaker, Bryant has
received more than four hundred awards and citations for
his work to empower low-wealth communities, including
Oprah Winfrey's Use Your Life Award, and was named a
"Community Hero" by *People* magazine on the tenth anni-
versary of the worst urban civil unrest in U.S. history. In
December 1994, Bryant was selected by *Time* magazine for
its "America's 50 Most Promising Leaders of the Future"
cover story.

Bryant received an honorary doctorate degree of human letters from Paul Quinn College of Dallas, Texas, and is the author of *Banking on Our Future*. He lives in Los Angeles with his wife, Sheila Jenine Kennedy Bryant, and their dog, Little Man.

**Mickey Butts** is an editor and writer in Berkeley, California. His writing has appeared in such publications as *Harvard Business Review*, the *McKinsey Quarterly*, the *Financial Times*, Portfolio.com, *Salon*, the *Industry Standard*, and *Wired*. He has collaborated on or edited such books as *Forces for Good*, *The Five Patterns of Extraordinary Careers*, *Strategic Alliances*, and *Mobilizing Generation 2.0*. He is a former editor of the *Industry Standard* and *Parenting* magazines. More information is at www.mickeybutts.com.

# INDEX

Jesus, 64
Jones, Quincy, 12, 39, 86, 163
Jordan, Michael, 116
Jurgensen, Jerry, 160

**K**

Kaye, Danny, 27
Kemp, Jack, 106
King, Rev. Dr. Martin Luther, Jr.:
Dr. Mays as "spiritual mentor"
of, 177; facing death, 40–41;
on having pride, 23; "I Have
a Dream" speech by, 40, 176;
influence of, 161, 162; on love
and respect, 121; as love leader,
64; on power of personal relationships, 87; wisdom of, 168
Kovacevich, Dick, 95–99
Kozlowsski, Dennis, 60
Krings, Frank, 65, 152–153

**L**

L.A. riots. *See* South Central
riots (1992)
Ladder builders, 123–124
Laden, Osama bin, 64
LaGuardia Community College,
159
Laughter, 133
Leaders: failure through fear, 11,
55–73; five love leadership laws
about, 11–12; as ladder builders, 123–124; loss as creating,
11, 21–53; servant leadership
by, 141–145, 160
Leading from loss law: advantage
provided through loss for,
43–46; author's personal experience with, 26–29; description
of, 11; drawing strength from

loss and, 29–33; family home
loss story of, 21–24
Lewis, C. S., 157
Lightner, Candice, 34
Lincoln, Abraham, 64
Lizárraga, David, 164–165
Los Angeles riots (1992), 46–53,
172
Los Angeles Unified School District, 121, 163
Loss: advantages gained through,
43–46; stories of leaders gaining wisdom through, 34–43;
strength forged through, 30–31;
three ways to respond to, 31–33
Love: as antidote to fear, 5, 73;
caring for others goal as guided
by, 78–79, 84–104; comparing
qualities of fear and, 8–9; crucial difference between fear and,
81–84; doing good goal as
guided by, 79, 104–107; indifference as opposite to, 106,
172; love leadership context of,
10; nature of, 56
Love leadership: *agape* (love)
definition of, 10–12; birth of
formalized philosophy of, 8–10;
discovering concept of, 5–10;
examples of practice of, 13–15;
legacy offered by, 18–19; long-
term relationships drive, 84–91;
problem solving through,
114–115; wealth as the reward
of, 106–107. *See also* Fear-based
leadership
Love leadership laws: fear fails,
11, 55–73; giving is getting, 12,
137–169; loss creates leaders,
11, 21–53; love makes money,

**199**